TO JOHN
THE BELOVED

ALICE GLEN

Review and Herald Publishing Association
Washington, D.C. 20012

Copyright © 1982 by the Review and Herald Publishing Association

This book was edited by
Thomas A. Davis
Designed by Howard Bullard
Illustrations by Elfred Lee
Text matter was set in 10 point Zapf

R & H Cataloging Service

Glen, Alice
　To John the beloved

　1. Bible.　N.T.　John—Commentaries.
I. Title.
　　　226.5

ISBN 0-8280-0160-X

PRINTED IN U.S.A.

Preface

The person who has been along a pathway a hundred times knows its significant features better than a stranger does. What a newcomer will miss, the old-timer may point out as singular, striking, novel, or historic. If we take a tourist bus over a mountain highway, the driver will sometimes suddenly stop. We wonder why; we can see nothing exceptional. But he suggests that we alight and follow him, and there, having pushed our way through scrub bush, we find a delightful lacy waterfall. Or back beyond the road we are suddenly halted by a grand panoramic view. Although the old-timer and the bus driver have been over the familiar territory many times, they enjoy coming back.

So, having read John's Gospel perhaps countless times, we are not bored by its familiarity. Rather, we are charmed by the fresh discoveries, the ever-new aspects we see. The later pages illumine what was perhaps a little dim in the earlier, and what we at first passed over hastily, we now stop to study with new eyes. For John's story is magnetic. One returns to its pages again and again with ever-increasing regard and renewed inquiry.

In telling a story, one can relate too little or too much. One can ruin it by severity or overstatement. John's story is simple with the simplicity of natural beauty, with the beauty of the natural heart. He did not intend to tell everything that he knew about Jesus. What guided him in his choice from his wealth of material is part of his book's impelling mystery.

Of John's Gospel one author has said:

> It is elemental, vital. Statements of profound truth crowd one upon another with axiomatic clearness and simplicity. Knowledge of the major facts of the birth and ministry of Christ is assumed. John steps to the heart of the significance of this Life that was manifested.*

But with this simplicity is a compression—and compression yields power. Take, for example, the symbols John introduces. They are symbols common not just to a few, but they are widely, perhaps universally, known. And each figure—Light or Bread or Water or Wine—opens up a world of related thoughts, a whole stream of meaning that we now connect to Christ. His story, then, is hinged not only to the past but to the present and coming generations.

Perhaps John has related altogether the events of less than

twenty-four days of our Saviour's life. When we consider that he was constantly with Him for three and a half years, John's account covers only about one day in fifty. What wonders did John behold that are untold in his Gospel? The other Gospels fill in some of the blanks. Yet only some. Their stories combined can portray only a portion of the marvels that centered in Jesus.

It was not indiscriminate choice that made John outline certain themes, but his genius called forth by love. He wrote not so much of public acts or sermons to the multitude, but sayings of Jesus far from the crowd, consultations with Jesus of which in some cases he was perhaps the only witness.

It seems strange that some of the high marks in the Saviour's life at which John was present are not mentioned by him, while he describes at length Jesus' conversation with a woman at a well or with a ruler who came to Him one night. Discussing the why of this could lead us far afield.

Ah, matchless John, so spiritually aware of a Saviour's grace and so apt a pupil of your divine Master, the same Lord who drew you to Himself guided your pen as you wrote His story. Your heart, moved by a great love and power caught from Him, flowed out through your pen in living pictures and words.

Oh, beloved John, where are the rest of those immemorial days you knew? Lost? Stored up, we believe, for the days of eternity, where all may sit at the feet of Him who lived those full days, and relive the glorious blessedness when men dwelt in the immediate presence of their Lord.

The following pages are not a scholarly treatise, but a few thoughts from meditations on John's Gospel, chiefly the first chapter, but sometimes overflowing into later ones.

---

* *The Bible Reader's Encyclopaedia and Concordance*, p. 214.

TO JOHN THE BELOVED

John first saw Jesus at the Jordan River. From that day John's life was never the same.

CHAPTER I

You set for yourself an impossible task at the beginning, John. You began a day-by-day biography of your Master from the time you met Him. Starting with His appearance at the River Jordan, you continued, *"The next day . . . ,"* * and that was the day *you* found Him—or He found you. Unforgettable days! So it is easy for you to carry on again with *"The next day . . ."* This was the day He decided to go to Galilee and the day of the momentous occasion when Philip and Nathanael were discovered. Your story continues, *"On the third day* there was a marriage at Cana in Galilee."

How could you hope to keep this up? How could you expect to relate each wonderful day in order? Yours was no robot mind of mechanical accuracy. Rather, with your pen uplifted, your mind ran off onto uncharted grounds. Overwhelmed by a flood of memories, you forgot your first purpose, and from your pen began to pour those wonderful accounts of some of the sayings and incidents in and around the life of your Lord.

Did you think you would give a diarylike record—this day, the next day, the third day, and on and on? Surely, John, you did not, or you could not have known yourself! How could you restrict yourself to mere outline, skeletal bareness, undressed scaffolding, when your pen became, as it were, charged with color? You, who at times could hardly write a fact without adding your own wonderfully illuminating comments, could not restrain the force of feeling that swept down onto your page. Because of these, your readers will sometimes be a little confused as to what is narrative and what is commentary.

For instance, early in the first chapter of your Gospel you introduce the Lord's forerunner, John the Baptist. "There was a man sent from God, whose name was John." But then you hurry by John to catch up with the One to whom he is pointing. "He came for testimony, to bear witness to the light." Now you are caught in the spell of that Light and have forgotten about the Baptist. Except for a parenthetical statement in verse 15, you do not return to your subject until verse 19.

Then, at last, having related how John the Baptist pointed his listeners to Jesus with that impressive metaphor that has lived down the ages, " 'Behold the Lamb of God, who takes away the sin of the world!' " you find the true theme of your pen, and the Baptist is forgotten for a while. You have found the Christ of your heart. All other scenes, events, or persons are not comparable with Him. Henceforth, whoever touches Christ touches your heart; His words, His acts, His expressions, are written there for memory to finger lightly or probe thoughtfully.

Is it any wonder, then, beloved John, that you do not continue your nice sequence with the ordered logic of one treating an indifferent subject? Are you to know that centuries later clouds of controversy will blow around your Gospel? Could you be coolly precise if you would be—with your burning heart and aching memories, your mind filled with wonder and praise?

Perhaps when you commenced your narrative, you meant to give a detailed account of the life of our Lord. But then your own particular style, the stroke of your own genius, took hold of your pen and swept it along in its own masterly manner. With the ease of a natural style your pen ran on, perhaps less with ink than the essence of the living Spirit. The soul overflowed the hand, as it were.

But you, John, were as we are, oh, so human, envisaging tasks beyond our performance, aiming at goals outside our fulfillment, reaching to unattainable dreams. In love and longing we outstretch ourselves. And when we fail—as so often we do in our endeavors—we look a little wryly at our poor attempts. Did you think you had failed, John, because you hadn't accomplished what you had set out to do?

I wonder how you viewed your finished work. Little, I imagine, did you realize your masterly achievement, your immortal performance. Did you know that you were giving your story to the ages, that what you wrote would be living bread to the coming generations? Could you, a humble fisherman, ever imagine you had produced an incomparable work of art? But, then, your story was not just devised by the human mind; it was constrained by Love and related by Truth. It was the offspring of an impassioned heart that, even in its great simplicity, knew it had had a unique experience, instinctively knew itself as a chosen vessel, and was therefore Spirit-driven to preserve for others that which all were meant to share.

So often God chooses a humble instrument to write His message, like Jeremiah, who said, "'I am only a youth'" (Jer. 1:6), or Amos, who declared, "'I am no prophet, nor a prophet's son; but I am a herdsman, and a dresser of sycamore trees, and the Lord took me from following the flock, and the Lord said to me, "Go, prophesy to my people Israel"'" (Amos 7:14, 15). Or like that mother of a great eighteenth-century reformer who is said to have turned back the tides of evil in his country. John Wesley's mother said, "I never durst positively presume to hope that God would make use of me as an instrument in doing good; the farthest I ever durst go was, It may be; who can tell?"

The fact that when the other Gospels were spreading, you did not rush in with your version, your account, but waited to write until you were an old man, when certain conditions and heresies in the church created the need of an authoritative statement such as you could best supply, reveals your humility. Then, according to accounts, urged by friends or at the request of the bishops of Asia, you sat down and gave your story. That may have been the motivation, but the execution, I think, was of divine compulsion.

But it was *your* story, and I wonder how the finished product pleased your fellow elders. Was it just what they had expected? Or did they grumble because you had not met their expectations? Were they as disappointed as in later centuries were the sitters who had commissioned Rembrandt to paint *The Night Watch*, failing to see in the finished picture the painter's immortal greatness?

But of your Gospel's endurance and power, would not you have been amazed and thrilled that a noted twentieth-century poet should write this strongly?

TO JOHN THE BELOVED

Not ev'n the Apostles, in the days
    They walked with Christ, lov'd Him so well
As we may now, who ken His praise
    Reading the story that they tell,
Writ by them when their vision grew.

—Robert Bridges

---

* The Scripture quotations not otherwise specified in this book are from the Revised Standard Version of the Bible, copyrighted 1946, 1952 © 1971, 1973.

CHAPTER II

"In the beginning . . ."

It seems so incongruous, John, that you, who were to write with what at times would seem to be such unpredictable abandon, should begin your narrative so neatly, so precisely, so logically with "In the beginning." In the beginning. Of course! Where else could you begin the story of your timeless Lord?

From our knowledge of your humility, we know you were setting up no rival to that book of beginnings, Genesis, whose first words are "In the beginning God." Yet, steeped as you were in the sacred writings, perhaps you instinctively patterned your record after that which told of the first Adam.

Even if there were some recognition of, or deliberation over, what you were doing, you would, we imagine, joyfully reflect that you were writing the story of the second Adam, and that it was fitting therefore that you should borrow the few striking introductory words of the book of beginnings.

Perhaps lodged within your breast was that secret knowledge that later educators would instill into their student teachers: "Hinge the unknown to the known." And just as present-day writers call their readers to attention by an apt and familiar quotation from one such as the great Shakespeare, so you evoke a living interest in your readers by the well-known phrase "In the beginning." Strangely, today some who claim to be atheists quote the Bible or call on God's name, perhaps to get people's attention.

And, by starting that way, you are carrying your Hebrew

"In the beginning" was the Creative Fiat, the Word, who spoke all things into existence.

TO JOHN THE BELOVED 13

readers along with you. The Genesis story is about the creative fiat, that Divine Word who brought all things into existence. You, John, with all your countrymen, knew well that familiar narrative. So very well known, too, were the psalmist's words "By the word of the Lord were the heavens made; and all the host of them by the breath of his mouth. . . . For he spake, and it was done; he commanded, and it stood fast" (Ps. 33:6-9, K.J.V.).

The mystery of God's creative power is inherent in those words "In the beginning God created." They hold the secret of all the unfathomable knowledge of this world and all the wonders that art and science can reveal.

In spite of the ancients' plethora of gods, were there some people in your day, John, teaching, "In the beginning God was not"? Had you the faintest conception that the idea of the beginning of the world and man without God, of living matter having arisen from nonliving matter, would become almost universal in civilization? Surely you could not guess that a vast and wonderful system explaining this world's growth would be worked out—a process called evolution—in which God would have no mention. This system would teach that plants and animals have existed on this planet for uncounted millions of years and in an order of sequence that geologists have studied out and know accurately, and that man himself has existed for more than a million years.

> Throughout the years, men have sought by reasoning to answer the questions of origin, duty, and destiny. The heathen have imagined that some fanciful man or beast or rock or star was the parent of all things earthly. . . .
>
> Many presumably educated men have endeavored to develop what they thought to be a more rational form of philosophy, and have postulated that the material of the earth—in fact, of the entire universe—always existed. . . . Still other men have presumed that there is or was a God of creation, but that He contented Himself with forming the building stuff possessed of unlimited developmental ability, and forthwith abandoned it to its own devices for elaboration and organization. . . .
>
> Other groups of individuals have endeavored to identify God with nature and thus have ignored entirely His personal attributes of omniscience and purposefulness, of benevolence, love, and justice.[1]

How much nearer to your sentiments would be the words

written many centuries after your time by one given to much meditation:

> The great secret of scripture is: in the beginning—God. In the beginning all that was, was God: now and forever, all that is, is God.... His Being is perfect; His understanding is infinite. His strength enables us to mount up as the eagle. His joy overflows our cup. Let us acknowledge His joy, His health, His understanding, His peace, His harmony, His purity, and His integrity.[2]

The same writer speaks of the world's creation in this way:

> Every blessing upon this earth is an emanation or an expression of God and God's law: the sun that warms us and the rain that feeds our plants and trees. The stars, the tides, and the moon all fulfill functions of God and yet appear as blessings to man. It could have been no accident that God hung the sun up in the sky, millions of miles away from the earth, just far enough away to give us the proper amount of warmth and the right amount of coolness. God really is the intelligence of this universe—an intelligence full of love and wisdom....
>
> God is the source of all that is. God's love is made evident in the fact that before man appeared on earth, everything was here necessary for his development, for his growth, and for his welfare. Even the minerals in the earth were given for man's use.[3]

When men ignore divine revelation and seek by intellect alone to penetrate the eternities of past and future, they are on unsure ground. In the early 1960s a team of top scientists advanced a new theory on the origin of the universe. The leading professor said he had cross-checked the findings ceaselessly during the previous two years and would challenge scientists throughout the world to find errors. The theory is that there had been a definite beginning to the universe and that it will not last forever.

But their belief contradicts the steady-state theory. Under the steady-state theory, announced in 1948 by Professor Fred Hoyle and two other Cambridge astronomers, the universe is everlasting, with no beginning and no end. Professor Hoyle said that his objection to believing that his theory was now disproved was a mathematical one, a newspaper report stated.

Time has gone on, and new discoveries force scientists, often reluctantly, to review findings. Now the big-bang theory is held as irrefutable. "Supporters of the steady-state theory have tried desperately to find an alternative explanation, but they have failed.

Now the big-bang theory has no competitors," wrote Robert Jastrow.

We are now informed that the earth is not as ancient as we have been told:

> Three astronomers say the discovery of a mistake in the way distances in space are measured means that the universe is only about half as old and half as big as they previously thought. The scientists who noticed the apparent error say the universe is only 9,000 million years old, not 15,000 or 18,000 million years, the usually accepted figures.[4]

Yet even today a change is taking place in the assessment of staunchly held theories. Dr. James H. Jauncey has written a book entitled *Science Returns to God*. The author is well able to write comprehensively on such a subject; besides filling eminent professional positions, he holds ten degrees in such subjects as science, psychology, philosophy, history, mathematics, and religion. His first chapter begins:

> It is now some thirty years since I was in undergraduate school. During that time, I have remained fairly close to developments in science; yet I never cease to be amazed at the tremendous change in outlook during this period. When I was in school, the general outlook of scientific people was frankly hostile to religion. As a matter of fact, it was frequently pointed out that unless the young student abandoned these religious superstitions, he could not hope to progress in scientific achievement.
>
> Now the situation is entirely different. The atheist or the hostile agnostic, even in scientific circles, is becoming a rare bird indeed. For a number of years I have been receiving invitations to speak on religion and science on many campuses throughout the land. The general attitude is always sympathetic and often very devout. This extends not only to the belief in God but also to belief in the Bible.[5]

Who will have the final word? A simpe faith clinging to its "thus saith the Lord" (K.J.V.) has a more sure and enduring foundation than a belief that is tossed around by the theories of even the most clever of men. Can the instruments of the skillful surgeon probing among a man's organs reveal his personality, character, or powers? Neither can the most dazzling wonders of astronomy or the astonishing findings of mathematics discover the hidden things of the Infinite, no matter how earnestly sought.

No, John, the theories of the cleverest of earth's men can never make you old-fashioned. The truth of the divine fiat cannot be disproved—"In the beginning God."

They have tried, of course. A perceptive writer of the early part of the century recognized the trend and wrote succinctly:

> The great facts of creation as presented by the inspired writers ... are practically rejected, either wholly or in part, by a large share of the professedly Christian world. Thousands who pride themselves upon their wisdom and independence, regard it an evidence of weakness to place implicit confidence in the Bible; they think it a proof of superior talent and learning to cavil at the Scriptures, and to spiritualize and explain away their most important truths.[6]

But you, John, happily unheeding of criticism and doubts and firmly assured in your attested belief, began with a simplicity that would not deter a child: "In the beginning was the Word." How far removed is your style from that of one who wrote of evolution as

> the integration of matter and concomitant dissipation of motion, accompanied by a continuous change, from indefinite incoherent homogeneity to a definite coherent heterogeneity, with structure and function, during which the retained motion undergoes a parallel transformation,

and which another interprets as

> a change from a nohowish untalkaboutable all-alikeness to a somehowish and in general talkaboutable not-all-alikeness by continuous something-else-ifications, and stick-together-ations.

Your simplicity and clarity lend conviction to your words, and in another place you express a much stronger affirmation of your Lord's eternity not only in the past but in the future: "I am Alpha and Omega, the beginning and the end," says the Lord (Rev. 22:13, K.J.V.). He, then, is not only the Word of the past but the Way of the future.

Moreover, there is deep-rooted within humanity something that *likes going back*. Instinctively we crave to know that we are not merely islanded in time but are solidly bridged to the past. The future is misty before us; then let us unveil the past. So scholars write histories, societies keep archives, organizations amass records, individuals pen biographies laying bare their own or others' family trees, geologists scan rocks, anthropologists analyze man, biologists probe the source of life, all to interpret the present

TO JOHN THE BELOVED 17

in the terms of the past, to keep it from drifting into annihilation and to hand it on as a heritage to the future.

And in our traveling the road of the past, our supreme pleasure is to arrive at the very *origin*, for in an origin there is a creative center. What compulsion or impelling force started something on its way? Who were the original characters, and what was their drive? What? Who? Why? How? When?

An origin holds at its center a unique germ of life; no future development, no matter how forceful or accomplished, can claim its distinction. Though later processes may overshadow it, it alone is preeminent in its badge of originality.

Today people who have been adopted in early childhood are claiming the right to know their real parentage, and organizations have been formed endorsing their claim and assisting them in finding their true parents.

Repeatedly, with mingled pride, admiration, wonder, and perhaps envy, we go back to the pioneer, discoverer, inventor, designer, founder, author, or merely the first of some line. Something broke through in these beginners, and though later men build upon their work, dwarfing with massive structures their tiny start, they are still the point at which all searching back will end. They are the beginning, the first of a notable line.

And yet, is the drift so wide between then and now? The poet found it

> Lovely and sweet and touching unto tears,
> That through man's chronicled and unchronicled years,
> And even into that unguessable beyond
> The water-hen has nested by a pond,
> Weaving dry flags into a beaten floor,
> The one sure product of her only lore. . . .
>
> Yes, daw and owl, curlew and crested hern,
> Kingfisher, mallard, water-rail and tern,
> Chaffinch and greenfinch, wagtail, stonechat, ruff,
> Whitethroat and robin, fly-catcher and chough,
> Missel-thrush, magpie, sparrow-hawk and jay,
> Built, *those far ages gone, in this year's way*. . . .

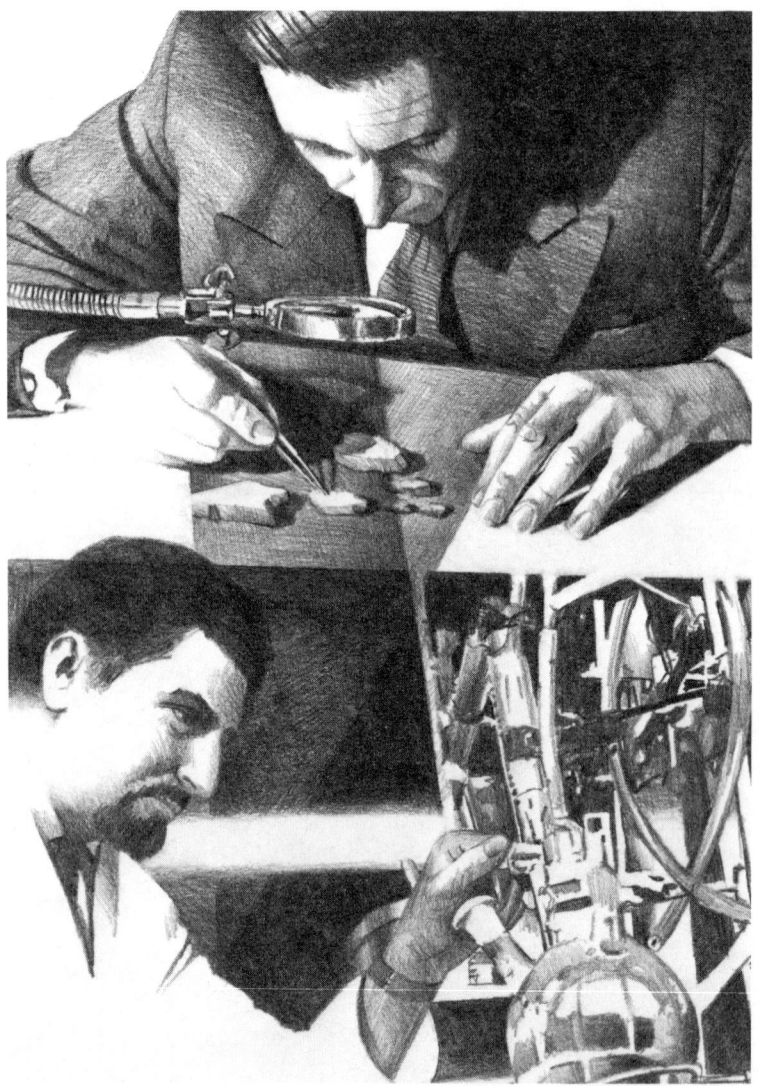

Man likes to go back to his origins, so scientists and historians scan the vestiges of the past.

> O delicate chain over all the ages stretched,
> O dumb tradition from what far darkness fetched:
> Each little architect with its own design
> Perpetual, fixed and right in stuff and line,
> Each little ministrant who knows one thing,
> One learned rite to celebrate the spring.
>
> Sir John Squire
(Italics supplied.)

And are there not other delicate chains "over all the ages stretched"? You, John, with one true, grand, and flawless span, arch the ages—"In the beginning was the Word." "The Word became flesh and dwelt among us."

---

[1] R. E. Hoen, *The Creator and His Workshop* (Mountain View, California: Pacific Press Publishing Association, 1951), pp. 1, 2.

[2] Joel S. Goldsmith, *The Art of Meditation* (New York: Harper & Brothers, 1956), p. 73.

[3] *Ibid.*, p. 66.

[4] Melbourne *Age*, 1979.

[5] (Grand Rapids: Zondervan Publishing House, 1971).

[6] Ellen G. White, *The Great Controversy* (Mountain View, California): Pacific Press Publishing Association, 1946, p. 583.

CHAPTER III

"In the beginning was the Word."

Well did you, John, root your words in the past with your "In the beginning"; then subtly you changed the focus of attention to the Word—the Logos.

> *The Word.* We need not ask whence this term came. It may have been a pebble from the brook of Old Testament Scripture, or a phrase borrowed, as Neander suggests, from the current talk of Ephesus, where this Gospel was written about the year A.D. 97. But, whencesoever it came, it is here reminted by the Spirit of God, and is most significant.[1]

As it has been pointed out, John, you wrote from Ephesus. And your problem

> was not the problem of presenting Christianity to the Jewish world; it was the presenting of Christianity to the Greek world. How then did this idea of the Word fit into Greek thought? In Greek thought the idea of the Word was there waiting to be used.... Away back in 560 B.C. there was an Ephesian philosopher called Heraclitus.... Heraclitus held that in the world of nature and events "all things happen according to the Logos," and that in the individual man "the Logos is the judge of truth." To Heraclitus the Logos was nothing less than the mind of God controlling this world and controlling every man.
>
> Once the Greeks had discovered this idea they never let it go. It fascinated them....
>
> In Alexandria there was a Jew called Philo.... No man ever knew the Jewish scriptures as he knew them; and no Jew ever knew the greatness of Greek thought as Philo knew it. He too knew and used and loved this idea of the Logos, the Word, the Reason of God....
>
> So Greek thought knew all about the Logos."[2]

We have this thought stated again by one who, rather than a theologian, is a word craftsman:

> The Stoics . . . gradually burdened the little Greek word "logos" with the weight of a whole metaphysical theory of the relation between spirit and matter. "Logos" in Greek had always meant both "word" and the creative faculty in human beings—"reason," as it is often translated—which expresses itself by making and using words. The Stoics were the first to identify this human faculty with that divine Mind which earlier Greek philosophers had perceived as pervading the visible universe. . . . Though he had never heard of Christianity, Philo, importing into the theory a certain Semitic awfulness, actually called this mysterious "logos" the "only-begotten son."
>
> Followers of Philo and his school saw in the Christ the Logos itself incarnate in human form, the Word made Flesh.[3]

And so, John, in your very first few words you neatly captured the attention of both your Jewish and Greek readers. Also, you have struck a familiar note with all your hearers, for all peoples, even the most primitive, have words, and he who is inarticulate (unless, of course, he is dumb) is hardly reckoned human.

For Helen Keller, the deaf-blind woman of genius, the joyful discovery of life started when she began to understand the meaning of words:

> I say, the *word* dropped from the fingers of another filtered through the closed doors of sense and filled my mind with light—the light of thought and understanding.[4]

Words are the common coin of speech, of which currency even the poorest has his store. Or, to change the figure, words are tools to put into shape a man's thoughts and ideas and to fashion them according to his capacity and will. Or, again, they are weapons to be sheathed in silence or wielded; some use them crudely as a blunt knife, others skillfully as a two-edged sword.

Perhaps, John, you knew some of the scriptural generalizations:

"How forcible are right words!" (Job 6:25, K.J.V.).

"A word spoken in due season, how good is it!" (Prov. 15:23, K.J.V.).

"A word fitly spoken is like apples of gold in pictures of silver"

(chap. 25:11, K.J.V.).
We all know something of their power:

A careless word
May kindle strife;
A cruel word
May wreck a life.

A bitter word
May hate instil;
A brutal word
May smite and kill.

A gracious word
May smooth the way;
A joyous word
May light the day.

A timely word
May lessen stress;
A loving word
May heal and bless.

—Grenville Kleiser

Lord Byron knew something of this power:

But words are things, and a small drop of ink,
Falling like dew upon a thought, produces
That which makes thousands, perhaps millions, think.

What words we could write and speak about words; but let us notice one epitome of their gracefulness:

God wove a web of loveliness,
   Of clouds and stars and birds,
But made not anything at all
   So beautiful as words.

They shine around our simple earth
   With golden shadowings,
And every common thing they touch
   Is exquisite with wings.

There's nothing poor and nothing small
   But is made fair with them.
They are the hands of living faith
   That touch the garment's hem.

—Anna Hempstead Branch[5]

And He who was called the Word had the gift of their magic. He held His hearers spellbound, and they "wondered at the gracious words which proceeded out of his mouth" (Luke 4:22). " 'No man ever spoke like this man!' " (John 7:46) said they who had come to arrest Him and had gone away convinced by His words. "He speaks with authority" was the summing up of others of His listeners. Words were both His miraculous rod and His two-edged sword.

But to return to your words, John, surely you knew some of the laws of the mind's working, something of the power of repetition and emphasis in imprinting facts upon the memory.

A nineteenth-century philosopher said that God and little children love monotony; hence the constant multiplication of Nature's processes and cycles, and of little children's rhymes and games. Perhaps, as between children and God, saints also never tire of certain repetitions. You, John, put it all so clearly and with such well-chosen emphasis and repetition that we cannot mistake your intention:

> In the beginning was the Word,
> > and the Word was with God,
> > and the Word was God.
>
> He was in the beginning with God;
> > All things were made through him;
> > and without him was not anything made
> > > that was made.

Whoever the Word is, He is the subject of your story. But there is something more that we must notice of the words in your first chapter. Your style, judged by our standards today, almost strikes a note of authority in its spare use of adjectives. You don't color things or "write them up" even with such simple descriptions as "good," "bright," "high." You speak of "life," "light," "darkness." Each stands absolute, a force in itself, entirely or almost a symbol. To describe one of these words would be to weaken it—except that you must distinguish between "true light" and the counterfeit light.

How different from today, when our speech is overladen with most vivid descriptions! While my mind was on these thoughts a

Light, water, bread—these are symbols that remind us of the Master.

newspaper article by a university professor, in which he satirizes our use of high-sounding terms, came to my notice. *"It's 'Terrific,' It's 'Titanic,'"* he heads his article on the abuses of adjectives, and cites some of them:

> A Unique Opportunity both Stupendous and Sensational. Unparalleled, Unexampled, Unheard-of, Unimaginable—these and many other "uns" are used so recklessly that they have lost all meaning. Visionary, e.g., a Visionary Bathroom. This is evidently a variant of Dream used as an adjective—e.g., a Dream-kitchen or a Dream-home. . . . I have a note, too, of a Voluptuous Bathroom. I should like this much better than a visionary one.

Fortunately this professor has a sense of humor and can view with amusement the extremes to which language can be taken.

But John's Gospel, which is peeled to the very core, creates a sense of fundamental reality. One is reminded of the passage from the sixteenth-century writer Montaigne:

> It is a pity that men of understanding are so fond of brevity. . . . Plutarch would rather have us applaud his judgment than his knowledge; he prefers to leave us not satiated, but still hungry for more. He knew that even on the greatest subjects too much can be said.

But that this is not the only style in which you can write, John, we can prove by reading some verses in the first chapter of one of your other books, Revelation (verses 12-16). How vivid are your descriptions there—*golden* lampstands, *long* robe, *golden* girdle, hair *white as wool, white as snow,* and so on. But there you are giving a detailed picture of your Lord as He appeared in His glorious temple.

In the Gospel perhaps is revealed something of the quality of your work when you are writing of ultimate and universal things rather than of comparative. With men there is good wine and poor wine, true witnesses and false witnesses, bright light and dim light. But your Master was Light, Water of Life, Bread of Life, and the prototype of many other symbols. Only sometimes will you need to define superlative qualities by such terms as eternal life and living water. But there is no extravagance of speech such as we know today, which falsely glamorizes much that is unworthy, tawdry, or at least superficial. Rather, yours is a style of understatement, that the essential qualities might shine through.

Nowhere in the Bible shall we find such clear and distinct statements about our Lord Jesus Christ's divine nature. Nowhere shall we find so many expressions, which for want of mental power, no mortal man can fully grasp or explain. In no portion of Scripture is it so deeply important to notice each word, and even each tense employed in each sentence. In no portion of Scripture do the perfect grammatical accuracy and verbal precision of an inspired composition shine out so brightly. It is not, perhaps, too much to say, that not a single word could be altered in the first five verses of St. John's Gospel, without opening the door to some heresy.[6]

But, then, you wrote of the *Word*, with whom none is comparable.

---

[1] F. B. Meyer, *Gospel of John* (Fort Washington, Pennsylvania: Christian Literature Crusade, Inc., 1970), p. 12.

[2] William Barclay (ed.), *The Gospel of John* (Philadelphia: Westminster Press, 1958), vol. 1, pp. 11-13.

[3] Owen Barfield, *History in English Words* (London: Faber & Faber, Ltd., 1962), pp. 113-115.

[4] Helen Keller, *The World I Live In* (London: Methuen & Co., Ltd., 1933).

[5] *High Tide* (London: Gerald Duckworth & Co., Ltd.).

[6] J. C. Ryle, *Ryle's Expository Thoughts on the Gospels* (Grand Rapids: Zondervan Publishing House, 1951), vol. 3, p. 6.

CHAPTER IV

*"In the beginning was the Word,
and the Word was with God,
and the Word was God.*

"He was in the beginning with God."

For impressing a fact upon the mind, John, you seemed to know a few of the rules. Is there any difference between the first sentence and the second sentence? Very little, it seems to me. But at least the repetition gives emphasis. And what was it you wished to emphasize? That in the beginning the Word was God and was with God.

Now, could you, John, have advanced nearly 1,900 years and placed the first verse before some theologians of today, possibly you would have observed them pouncing upon the phrase "In the beginning," and with casuistry claiming that there wasn't a beginning—or if there was a beginning, when was it? And in all the conjecture and examination this short verse would arouse, one small word would very likely be overlooked—yet how important it is!

Could you have transported yourself through time to a modern schoolroom where the English language is being taught to 9- and 10-year-olds, you, John, might have seen a practical illustration of that one seemingly insignificant word used.

The teacher is endeavoring to teach the class the meaning and use of prepositions, those little useful words that show relationships. Taking a book, she puts it on the table and writes on the blackboard, "The book is *on* the table." She then places the book underneath the table and elicits that "the book is *under* the table." She puts the book *in* a drawer, *beside* a ruler, and so on.

But when she comes to the little preposition *with*, she feels a more personal illustration is needed, and she says, "a visitor is *with* our class today." Thus, John, you are drawn within the group as one of its members. You are no mere observer, a mere stranger. The little word *with* has opened up hospitable implications and a warm intimacy. In important respects you are part of this young group climbing the difficult ladder of language.

And in your precious Gospel the word *with* carries remarkable associations and revealing ties of close relationship. Twice you said it in those first two verses, with one swift stroke summing up the preearthly life of your Lord. Now it is left to human imagination or further divine revelation to clothe the mind with the picture.

"No one has ever seen God," you wrote in verse 18.

"'You cannot see my face,'" God had told Moses, "'for man shall not see me and live'" (Ex. 33:20). Moses, who talked with God, was unable to see more than the trail of His glory from a cleft in a rock. But even so, when Moses came down from the mount, the children of Israel could not bear the shining of his face.

Yet, beloved apostle, you said your Lord had had His habitation *with* God and was Himself God. How perfect, how holy, must that Lord have been! He dwelt *with* Him who was eternal, immortal, invisible—the Omniscient, Omnipotent One. Our minds fall away from the contemplation of His greatness. You were wise, John, to limit your pen so admirably.

It is just as well that, a lttle later, you make the startling revelation "The Word became flesh and dwelt among us," for that brings us from the place where we cannot go, even in imagination, to reality. We are sinful and mortal, and the perfect, pure, and exalted Being who is God is high and lifted up beyond our eyes.

Men have wanted to know God and what He is like, and they have tried through art forms to make some representation of Him. Their worst attempts were grim idols and less-than-human images, and their best—well, men have daringly attempted the impossible, even to the point of causing their fellow men to bow in awe and reverence.

"The Word was *with* God." Here is a mysterious unity, incomprehensible to man's searching mind. That was before your time, chosen disciple, back in the days known to us as B.C., for that is all that you, and we, can comprehend—time, not eternity. And B.C. indicates a line drawn through time. Now comes the period when your personal story swings into focus.

And what have you to say on that momentous, that never-to-be-forgotten, ever-to-be-remembered day that began your new life, that day when Jesus first turned and looked at you, saying, "'What do you seek?'"

Not knowing what else to say, you replied, "'Rabbi . . . , where are you staying?'"

"'Come and see,'" He said, giving a gracious invitation.

Then, the story continues, you went, saw where He was staying, and "stayed *with* him that day."

Here was introduced to you the wonderful plan by which divinity could more and more overflow to man. A friendship was established. Christ was a new link between heaven and earth. When man's grip of that link was strong, he was strong; when his grip of it was weak, he was weak. Of its strength and weakness you, John, gave evidence later in your Gospel.

On that fatal night in the Garden, your story says, "Jesus . . . went forth *with* his disciples" (chap. 18:1). The little circle was complete except for the traitor. And he? When the soldiers and officers penetrated the sacred precincts, "Judas, who betrayed him, was standing *with* them" (verse 5). How keenly indeed is that little word *with* here portrayed as one of relationship.

And when Jesus' group was broken up and scattered, that word *with* poignantly reveals another sad breaking of the close unity of the Master and His apostles. The story continues in John 18:18: "Now the servants and officers had made a charcoal fire, because it was cold, and they were standing and warming themselves; Peter also was *with* them, standing and warming himself." Peter, in appearance at least, was on the other side, which led him to behave as if he were actually in sympathy with Jesus' enemies.

Now Jesus was quite alone. No longer could His friends be with Him. The nearest they could get—and you yourself were there, beloved friend, with Mary, Jesus' mother—was *by* the cross of

At the cross John stood with Mary the mother of Jesus, and watched Him suffer—alone.

Jesus. No one could be *with* Him on the cross. Even God, it seemed, had forsaken Him. "I have trodden the winepress alone; and of the people there was *none with me*" (Isa. 63:3, K.J.V.). This was one of the terrible mysteries of Christ's passion.

Afterward you had a story to tell about Thomas in the upper room (John 20:24-29). When Jesus first appeared to His disciples after His resurrection, "Thomas, one of the twelve, called the Twin, was *not with* them." He refused to believe them when they said, "'We have seen the Lord.'" But "eight days later, his disciples were again in the house, and Thomas was *with* them." Again Jesus came and stood among them, and said, "'Peace be *with* you.'" He then turned and addressed Himself especially to Thomas, saying, "'Put your finger here, and see my hands; and put out your hand, and place it in my side; do not be faithless, but believing.'" Thomas, of the bold assertions, was crushed, and in awe could only murmur, "'My Lord and my God!'"

It is obvious what amazed and humbled Thomas. None of the disciples had seen Jesus since that other encounter at which Thomas was not present. How did Jesus know the bitter words of unbelief he had expressed when they told him about Jesus' mystic visitation? "'Unless I see in his hands the print of the nails, and place my finger in the mark of the nails, and place my hand in his side, I will not believe,'" he had said. How did Jesus know? He must then have been present *with* them! Thomas would assent only to visible evidence of the flesh. Jesus, in giving this evidence, provided the fact of a spiritual mystery. Jesus, invisibly present, had been *with* them. The doubter was convinced. He was convinced because of the physical evidence Jesus had supplied. "Jesus said to him, 'Have you believed because you have seen me? Blessed are those who have not seen and yet believe.'"

Did Jesus expect people to believe before having proper, convincing evidence? Why was Thomas gently rebuked for requiring proofs of the Lord's resurrection? I think, John, your text supplies two answers. Thomas had failed to recognize two sources of evidence.

First, he had swept aside the witness of his brethren; he gave no credence to their story. Ah, he had already been "duped" enough, and they were all the laughingstock of the city. Did they expect him to believe some ghost story to make them a further butt of scorn? He, for one, was discredited enough in the eyes of family, friends, and foes alike to wish not to make himself look a worse fool. Nothing but the strongest evidence of his own good senses would satisfy him. And just to *see* some figment wouldn't be enough, either, for the eyes could be duped into imagining a fantasy. His very hand would have to assure him by contact with those terrible wounds that, in his mind's eye, were still bleeding. They were closely connected with much of his present misery and agony. Nothing less than the touch of them would convince him.

In nursing his own quivering grief, Thomas failed to accredit the other apostles with being stricken as badly as he. He did not stop to recognize that they had as good cause as he for wishing not to fall easy victims of a grand deception. Possibly his own sorrow blinded him to that of the others.

So Thomas had come among his brethren with a spirit that brought discord and disillusionment—and so he had left them. He hadn't given his friends a chance. Had he but quieted his bitterness he might have discerned a strange atmosphere among these men whose Master had so recently been murdered. There was a peace and joy in the midst of them. Thomas utterly missed this second piece of evidence that his risen Lord was actually *with* them. It was almost as if He were hiding behind a screen. Maybe He would have stepped out if Thomas had waited to give more credence to the others' story.

And concerning Thomas, I am glad, John, for that lovely lakeside cameo of gold and blue that follows on so closely in your story. "After these things Jesus shewed himself again to the disciples at the sea of Tiberias; and on this wise shewed he himself. There *were together* Simon Peter, and Thomas called Didymus, and Nathanael of Cana in Galilee, and the sons of Zebedee, and two other of his disciples" (chap. 21:1, 2, K.J.V.). Yes, this time, although they all were not there, Thomas was *with* them.

I am glad, too, beloved apostle, for what I believe was the sequel to your Gospel, which you wrote after seeing the vision of your Lord in heaven. (Scholars, I know, are not sure which was written first.) Oh, it was your Lord all right. The words He gave to you were redolent with His own unintruding graciousness and warm hospitality:

> Behold, I stand at the door, and knock: if any man hear my voice,

and open the door, I will come in to him, and will sup *with* him, and he *with* me. To him that overcometh will I grant to sit *with* me in my throne, even as I also overcame, and am set down *with* my Father in his throne" (Rev. 3:20, 21, K.J.V.).

Leslie Weatherhead has written of it thus:

> That God is *with us* seems to me the golden thread of comfort and sustenance that runs throughout the Bible from beginning to end.... Jesus Himself, we note, was never a recluse....

"I will ... give you another Comforter," said Jesus, "that he may be *with you* for ever." *"With you"*—the words are like a lovely haunting refrain that occurs through all the music of the Bible message.
"Behold," the poet prophet had declared,
"a virgin shall conceive, and bear a son,
and shall call his name Emmanuel [which means,
"God is with us" (margin)]" (Isa. 7:14, K.J.V.).

CHAPTER V

"Without him was not anything made that was made."

The *Amplified Bible* renders this verse, "Without Him was not *even one thing* made that has come into being."[1]

This has always been so, from the first days when things were those of sea, land, and air, when there came into existence

> the mountains, God's thoughts piled up; the valleys, God's thoughts spread out; the rivers, God's thoughts in motion; the dewdrops, God's thoughts in pearl; the flowers, God's thoughts in bloom.—Sherman A. Nagel.

It is so even today, when the word *things* covers all these and the multitude of articles formed by the hands of man.

The perfection and wonder of those works directly created, though marred by sin, have shone through until now, when poets still eulogize them in exquisite language.

> Nature! whose lapidary seas
> Labour a pebble without ease,
> Till they unto perfection bring
> That miracle of polishing;
> Who never negligently yet
> Fashioned an April violet,
> Nor would forgive, did June disclose
> Unceremoniously the rose;
> Who makes the toadstool in the grass
> The carven ivory surpass,
> So guiltless of a fault or slip
> Is its victorious workmanship;

> Who suffers us pure Form to see
> In a dead leaf's anatomy;
> And pondering long where greenly sleep
> The unravished secrets of the deep,
> Bids the all-courted pearl express
> Her final thoughts on flawlessness.
>
> —Sir William Watson[2]

Since time's dawn, the earth's things have increased in number and complexity. Even classes of things today comprise exhausting lists. Yet "without Him was not even one thing made that has come into being."

You, John, were probably aware of some of the women's things mentioned in Isaiah:

> the finery of the anklets, the headbands, and the crescents; the pendants, the bracelets, and the scarfs; the headdresses, the armlets, the sashes, the perfume boxes, and the amulets; the signet rings and nose rings; the festal robes, the mantles, the cloaks, and the handbags; the garments of gauze, the linen garments, the turbans, and the veils (chap. 3:18-23).

For, after all, in all ages has not so much of the world's inventions and craft been for women's sake? You yourself made a list, a ravishing list, of the riches of the woman of Babylon:

> gold, silver, jewels and pearls, fine linen, purple, silk and scarlet, all kinds of scented wood, all articles of ivory, all articles of costly wood, bronze, iron and marble, cinnamon, spice, incense, myrrh, frankincense, wine, oil, fine flour and wheat, cattle and sheep, horses and chariots, and slaves" (Rev. 18:12, 13).

In the Scriptures are other lists of fine and costly things—for example, the beautiful and generous gifts the children of Israel made for the tabernacle. Exodus 35:22-29 is more than a mere catalog or summary from a long-ago trade journal, but a heart-stirring account of the way these people—"both men and women," "all the men and women, the people of Israel, whose heart moved them"—brought their freewill offering for the Lord's temple. It is just one of the stories of how things can be well and wisely used.

The splendor of the wealth of Solomon is there, who excelled all the kings of the earth in riches and in wisdom.

Archeologists today are finding the diverse things, both common articles and treasures of craftsmanship, that vanished civilizations have used and cherished. And through all generations the words hold true, "Without Him was not even one thing made that has come into being." For God gave men both outward gifts and their own physical skills, and even when they abuse and misapply them (God allowing men to exercise their power of choice), they are still His gifts they are using or misusing.

Today a man goes into a supermarket or department store and—in spite of his acquaintance with labor-saving devices, utilities, luxuries, sportsgoods, toys, and hosts of other products—he is amazed at the number and variety and design of human inventions. The store is only the central marketing place for these things. From where did they come? Following back through the tortuous ways of transport, he is led into a bewildering world of factories and is amazed by the intricacy and scope of the production lines. Here are mechanical workers whose functions at first glance are beyond his comprehension. These are the wonder children of men's inventions, and behind them stand more wonders still, the design and production of the machines and the story of the raw materials from which the goods themselves are processed.

All this is man's work, and in it men, women, and children delight. Its superabundance is staggering. Even the smallest contrivance was somebody's creation, and over the more intricate object a whole army of workers has sweat and toiled. For the invention, production, and distribution of civilized men's things, men and women give much of their lives.

Yet we may look at elegant furniture, the latest car, the newest refrigerator, the most recent plastic novelty, the glass-plated skyscraper, a new ingenious farm implement, some clever labor-saving kitchen gadget, the most exquisite frock or the latest synthetic fabric, or a host of other modern productions and still say, "Without Him was not even one thing made that has come into being." For He who made the substances with which man works, made also the mind with its power of ingenious invention and the hand with its skill. Whether man uses these powers well or ill is another matter.

Without discussing how much God is involved in men's

creations, we can appreciate the meditation of one character in John D. Sheridan's *God Made Little Apples*:

> The things that were Caesar's were not really Caesar's. Everything came from the Man above. He drew the blueprints, and looked over the shoulders of the planners. Toothbrushes and submarines were His, sleeping pills and radar, polar bears and teddy bears. Bathing caps and electric drills were no different from dogfish, and television was simply a putting together of components that He had hidden under stones for the finding.[3]

Yet here is an amazing paradox: He without whom "was not anything made that was made" came poor into this world.

> As Joseph was a-walking
>   He heard an angel sing:
> "This night there shall be born
>   Our heavenly King.
>
> "He neither shall be born
>   In housen, nor in hall,
> Nor in the place of Paradise,
>   But in an ox's stall.
>
> "He neither shall be clothèd
>   In purple nor in pall;
> But in the fair, white linen,
>   That usen babies all.
>
> "He neither shall be rockèd
>   In silver nor in gold;
> But in a wooden cradle
>   That rocks on the mould."
>
> —*Author Unknown*

Cradled in a lowly manger, Jesus left the world "empty-handed." His poverty at death was not because He had had no opportunity to obtain possessions. We know that the devil offered Him all the kingdoms of this world and that the people wished to make Him a king. Here is perhaps the most inspiring brief biography that has been written:

> Christ Jesus, who, though he was in the form of God, did not count equality with God a thing to be grasped, but emptied himself, taking the form of a servant, being born in the likeness of men. And being found in human form he humbled himself and became obedient unto death, even death on a cross (Phil. 2:5-8).

He who created the world began life in a manger and left the earth in material poverty.

So thoroughly did He strip Himself that He hung naked on the cross, His very clothes having been distributed to the soldiery. He had always so lived superior to the clamoring world of things that at last He possessed not one of those that He had created for the welfare and happiness of His creatures. As a man His needs were the same as those of other men. His flesh, like all flesh, responded to comfort or shrank from pain, yet He was unencumbered by any manner of possessions.

Here we touch upon a great mystery—the poverty of Christ. He—without whom was not one thing made of all the wonderful things created for man's well-being and happiness—denied Himself of all but the absolutely necessary. His complete detachment from the arrogance of things shines out as part of His perfection.

He, the divine Son of God, was absolutely unpossessed by material things. The One who must eventually dispossess the evil prince of this world from his usurpation must be superior to the tyranny of earthly possessions. In turning men away from the mighty power of this world, He demonstrated utterly that not to *get* but to *give* is the way of life in the kingdom of God. Having least, He gave mankind most; possessing nothing, He possessed all things.

Christ was a king who tasted the poverty of His lowest subjects. Only those who have lived with the down and out—the destitute, the underprivileged, the homeless, the hopeless, the starving, the unemployed—really know their lot, not merely the hardship, but the humiliation and the insidious inroads of squalor and degradation upon the personality, the morality, and the spirit of these people. A well-known journalist of another day assigned himself the role of living with the lowest for a time, but he had to abandon the project. The closeness to unwashed bodies (his own also unwashed), the hunger, the necessity of going to a public library even to see the daily newspaper—these and other indignities and inconveniences, together with the abject misery of it all, were more than this cultured man could bear.

Christ was a man, and as a man He understood the very depths of man's nature. One of the instincts deep in humanity is to possess. Temporal goods are a support and security even in a primitive community. Tribes of remote New Guinea, so backward as to have garments of bark, were found with their wealth of shell strings. To more civilized people worldly wealth is also a source of pride, prestige, and power.

The centuries could unfold countless stories concerning man's acquisitive and possessive nature. One of Britain's popular writers and radio speakers, Nancy Price, made some illuminating remarks on this human quality:

One day an old tramp walking ahead of her wearily dropped his bundle and sat down on a bank. She joined him, and they talked. A large car whizzing by and just missing his pack led to their talking about possessions.

> "The tramp said, 'I frequent occupies mesel' wi' puzzlin' out wat I can drop out o' they bundles. Then I travels lighter, see; but some foalk won't part wi' nowt as they once laid theer 'ands on.'
> "'You are wiser than most of us,' I said, and thought how, wandering over the Downs, or ambling through the village, talking with men of the road, dropping into cottages for a gossip or a cup of tea, I ever saw Possession, material and abstract, dominating. . . .
> "As I sat beside the old tramp I thought how wise he was to discard rather than collect or hold, but even as I did so, and in spite of what he said, I noticed how from time to time he clutched the bundle at his side."[4]

She thought of an old shepherd she had met:

> "As he fondled his old gnarled stick upon which he leaned, he said affectionately, 'Nowt counts to me but me old pal now.'
> "There is no doubt, discard as we may, we always cling to some possessions."[5]

Greed, acquisitiveness, pride, and ambition urge us to get. Upon this natural tendency, weak or strong, modern advertising, fabulous sweepstakes, the so-accessible gambling, radio and television handouts, the slick salesmen, and the investment market work insidiously, stirring up desire where it hardly exists, or fanning it into a bright flame where it is strong.

In gold-mining days some of the miners, when asked what they would do with gold if they found it, replied, "I don't know." They only knew they wanted it. Today some of those who win huge amounts at gambling or some such thing do not know what to do with their fortune. Some do not even spend it, but continue the

TO JOHN THE BELOVED

Men have many ways of pursuing wealth, but wealth cannot buy contentment.

same life style as previously. Others admit that wealth has brought them more unhappiness than contentment. Yet many winners still continue to buy tickets for another unneeded fortune. Such is the compelling lust of wealth.

Beloved John, against such an inherent quality that most of us must admit to, we have your picture of the divine Master, who gave us His selfless example and words: "Labour not for the meat which perisheth, but for that meat which endureth unto everlasting life" (John 6:27, K.J.V.). And your teaching, too, that tells us to "love not the world, neither the things that are in the world" (1 John 2:15, K.J.V.). We have your example (a type of all the apostles), also. One day when you and Peter were entreated by a poor blind beggar, Peter replied (you just as well could have said it), "Silver and gold have I none; but such as I have give I thee: In the name of Jesus Christ of Nazareth rise up and walk" (Acts 3:6, K.J.V.).

---

[1] From the *Amplified New Testament*. Copyright The Lockman Foundation 1954, 1958. Used by permission.
[2] "Nature's Way," *An Anthology of Modern Verse*.
[3] (New York: Farrar, Straus & Co., Inc., 1962), p. 157.
[4] *The Heart of a Vagabond* (London: Museum Press, Ltd., 1955).
[5] *Ibid.*

CHAPTER VI

"In him was life, and the life was the light of men. . . . The true light that enlightens every man was coming into the world."

Not yet, beloved scribe, do you abandon the age-old and revered pattern with which you started. The world's Creation begins with the grand drama of God sweeping away the great chaos of darkness: "The earth was without form and void, and darkness was upon the face of the deep; . . . and God said, 'Let there be light'" (Gen. 1:2, 3). Now we read, "In him was life, and the life was the light of men. The light shines in the darkness, and the darkness has not overcome it."

Yes, this is to be a story of darkness and light,

Darkness, the blind one;
Light, the million-tinted.

Long years after you, John, an immortal painter would arise of whom it would be said, "He paints the light that makes holiness even of the commonplace." Your Lord was to turn on the light in commonplace lives.

Centuries after your time artificial light would become so common and easily obtained as to illuminate a city at the turn of a switch. But still it would captivate and fascinate the human sense. Light! Bewildering, fascinating light! Drawing people by their eyes within the warmth of its dazzling circle to the heart of its glow!

Light in our day is so plentiful that one writes:

The whole space where my window was has become a modern

masterpiece, a landscape of light. . . . Looking out on my landscape night after night I am reminded of the remark made by a friend from a tiny French village on her first visit to the United States the night we sat up together on a southbound train from New York watching the endless lights across the New Jersey marshes. 'But so many lights,' she said. 'What for? You think these people wish to compete with the stars?' "—Barbara Beecher.

Daylight is always a beautiful, wonderful, and precious thing. When Light swung upon this world, Chaos fled and Darkness flung down its scepter, which the devil took up with a challenge.

You, John, lived in a day when once night had settled in, there was little to penetrate its realms. It could be an awful thing, even an evil thing. A flare, a taper, a lamp, might disperse it for a short time, for a meager space, but lights of all kinds were rare and mostly feeble.

Had you eyes to look down the centuries, what transformations you would have seen over the kingdom of darkness in the cities of men—light in brimming pools, in glorious streams, in glittering cascades. Yellow, red, green, and blue lights! Light that burned all night and on past the rising sun. Light spilling brilliantly from doorways, flowing out countless windows, beckoning from roofs and high hills. Flashing lights, blinking lights, lights twisted into animated shapes, lights in long tubes, lights that flick on and off—a bewildering, mystifying array of lights! Lights in such a spate as to dazzle and blind! A glorious victory of man over earth's dark night.

Yet maybe your anointed eyes, John, would perceive, besides the beauty and blessing, the blatant garishness of much of this brilliant show. A gaudy Las Vegas would not appeal to you, nor an overbright saloon, nor the harsh illumination of haunts of squalor and sin that night's shadows would do well to veil, nor the dazzling chandeliers of a fashionable nightclub. This, you would observe, is not "the true light." Man's light informs the eye—of what? It illuminates—for what purpose? It gives sight to the outward eye, but within, the soul of man is thrown into greater darkness. "The true light" is that which kindles the inner eye.

Light within the soul of man was eclipsed when his eyes were opened to evil in that Garden of long ago, and the darkness has intensified. When a city has a blackout, people may realize a little how indispensable to their way of life is artificial light. But to give light to mere outward sight is a weak palliative to a far greater need. Perhaps, John, within your own soul you had known the depths of darkness and had yearned for illumination. So you wrote of the True Light, "The light shines in the darkness, and the darkness has not overcome it. . . .

"The true light that enlightens every man was coming into the world," and you will set up this Light as a seat of judgment of man's inward soul. A man with one eye sees more than a caterpillar with five or a fly with hundreds. So the Light revealed to a man depends on the capacity of his inward vision. The Light is there, but some will not see Him and it; they are blind to its radiance and beauty.

Later on you would record His own illustrious declaration: " 'I am the light of the world; he who follows me will not walk in darkness, but will have the light of life' " (John 8:12).

But back to the beginning! Who was this Light of whom you are writing, John? So far you have not named Him. We scan the following words and read this amazing sentence: "He was in the world, and the world was made through him, yet the world knew him not."

Past tense! He came and went? Unrecognized? Unhonored? How could it be that He whom you call Light came and went as any insignificant person might come or go? Light is the life of the world; the sun is the master of the day, and all creation responds to its glorious rising. Surely also the souls of men would respond when their Sun arose! Yet they did not. It is incredible, and yet—and yet . . .

Men may shut themselves away in cells or underground caverns long enough so that when they emerge into daylight they do not welcome the beautiful golden light, but must close their eyes to its glare. When an Italian scientist, Dr. Giancarlo Masini, stepped into the daylight after only a week in a cave 2,624 feet underground, lit only by candles and incandescent lamps, he staggered from sudden blindness. The ordinary light of day hit his eyes with unbearable intensity and a dazzle of vivid colors.

There have been little "blind" pit ponies, those shut up in underground mines, whose eyes became so inured to constant darkness that if exposed to the daylight they became blind. And some humans become so habituated to "underground living" that they cling to that way of life.

Coober Pedy, South Australia, is the home of beautiful opals. Because of the wind and dust it is impossible to live above ground there, so the people live in dugouts. A visitor there has written:

> Many people have likened the whole of Coober Pedy to a graveyard, and certainly the honeycomb of holes in the ground looks like a freshly dug cemetery.[1]
>
> We visited other parts of the field and the shafts of many gougers and their wives. Some had made lots of money and mostly spent it all, and lived on in their dugouts. There were many who had struck just enough opal to be able to carry on living and eternally digging. Then there were others who collected their old-age pensions, and even invalid pensions, and lived out the rest of their days encased like troglodytes in the sands of the ancient sea, forgotten by the world, sometimes even forgotten by Coober Pedy itself.
>
> Once we found just one man in the field of deserted diggings. Not a sound came from hundreds of open shafts that lay all about him, gaping up to the sun. Only the sound of the wind howling across the mullock heaps and the clash of a door which had once been a neighbour's as it swung from a gaping hole in the hillside.[2]

Men can so draw about their hearts and minds shades of darkness that they become used to their stygian blackness and love its murky shades. They prefer the concealing dark to the revealing light. They invoke the deceptive shades and welcome the distorting shadows. They would rather grope in abysmal ignorance than attempt the hazards of the true path. They love confusion rather than clarity, dimness instead of daylight. Their works of darkness cannot endure the light.

It is plain, John, that your Light, in the spiritual sense, was not visible to the outward eye, for thus He would have forced Himself upon men's vision. He came to enlighten the inner eye. Later on, you would report Him telling some men who could see outward objects very clearly, very keenly and critically (particularly some things of which they disapproved), that they were worse than blind (see John 9:39-41). Their understanding was unseeing and uncomprehending. And the tragic fact was that they did not want to see. Nothing, not even the Light Himself, could make them see that against which they closed the shutters of their inward eyes.

Oh, how easy it is to close our inner eyes! We give no attention to that which we do not want to recognize, and so our consciousness (and our conscience) is uninformed. On the street we can deliberately "not see" people, and just as easily we can ignore an unwanted fact or rush away from an unpalatable truth. John, you must often have watched the faces of the crowd when your Master was talking. Did you sometimes notice people turn off their attention when they no longer wished to hear? If they couldn't remove themselves physically, generally their minds tried to busy themselves with something else. You knew the words were just rushing by them like the wind. Like seeds on the granite, they would get no farther.

Today we have a saying reportedly based on an incident involving a little boy who had a grudge against a hunter. To get revenge—the next time the hunter was out hunting and as soon as the hare had passed a spot where the boy had hidden himself—he drew a red herring across the track, climbed a concealing hedge, and ran across a field. When the hounds came to the herring's track, they left the path to pursue the herring, which led them on a long, fruitless hunt. So we talk of diverting attention from the main issue by drawing a red herring across the path, a ruse at which, oh, how many of us are adept!

> Not everyone is ready for the dawn;
> See how some gaze
> Upon this latest of our days
> With summer-sunset eyes.
> How others yawn,
> And many, wishing they could lie
> In bed an hour longer, sigh;
> Not everyone is ready for the dawn.
>
> Not everyone is happy in the light,
> And so accursed
> Is each new chain-reaction burst
> Of man-revealing sun.
> Preferring night
> Are those whose habits are the stark
> Unhallowed mysteries of the dark;
> Not everyone is happy in the light.
>
> —Ian Healy

All summer long the outside canopy blind has been drawn over the study windows. The room, though perhaps cool, has been dim and sepulchral. It has been neglected, abandoned, unless in

Watchers in the Arctic, seeing the first arc of the returning sun, exult in the first light.

urgency the electric light has been turned on. But artificial light on a sunny day seems a false and glaring thing.

Today the blind has gone up, and the glorious autumn sunshine pours through the window. Welcome, wholesome beams of radiant light! So glorious is the sunlight today that one seems almost an ingrate to be indoors. The highway buzzes with the stream of cars, and the air echoes with the sound of footsteps and voices. We have bathed the dog and watered the garden—any excuse serves us today to stay outside. The very air is a tonic, and the atmosphere in this glorious sunshine seems to pour into one something of the elixir of life. One feels something of perennial youth within. One's body is charged to action; one's mind is invigorated.

A million existences are kindled to abounding life, and there is joy in flower and tree, in bird and bush. Today earth's light, heaven's golden sun, unchallenged by so much as a cloud, undisputed by even a puff of a breeze, is pouring its benign flood upon the grateful earth. The instinct of every creature responds to this light, this boon of life.

So must it have been when the True Light came to earth and touched with His warm, gentle streams a harsh and frozen world. He brought sunshine and joy, healing and happiness. He melted frigid hearts and awoke sleeping minds to radiant consciousness. Like watchers in an Arctic winter, seeing the first arc of the returning sun, hearts burst with the news "The Light! The Light has come!"

Against the harsh and forbidding aspects of those northern lands—"forlorn, stern, austere"—Roger P. Buliard has set the beauty and appeal of its lights:

> You cannot but love our northern sky. Better than anything else, it expresses the quality of the country, for it is vast and limitless, the great sun riding high in summer, the North Star almost overhead at night. It is the sky filled with stars, filled with sun, that offers hope and beauty to the northern men.[3]

There is only one sun! A million million candles cannot outshine it, nor heavenly satellites be its deputy. There is also but one heavenly Son, for whom there is no stand-in.

> We may look up, and the sun as it rules the day will remind us of

the Sun of Righteousness, who desires to rule not only our days but also our lives. . . . Let us rejoice in the sunshine of God's love.[4]

[1] Charles and Elsa Chauvel, *Walkabout* (London: W. H. Allen & Co., Ltd.), p. 174.

[2] *Ibid.*, pp. 185, 186.

[3] *Inuk* (London: Macmillan & Co., Ltd., 1956), p. 51.

[4] Burton H. Phipps, *Day Unto Day* (Washington, D.C.: Review and Herald Publishing Assn., 1954), p. 11.

CHAPTER VII

"He was in the world, and the world was made through him, yet the world knew him not. He came unto his own home, and his own people received him not."

One Bible commentary observes that

> the language here is nearly as wonderful as the thought. Observe its compact simplicity, its sonorousness . . . and the enigmatic form in which it is couched, startling the reader and setting his ingenuity a-working to solve the stupendous enigma of *Christ ignored in His own world.**

Here the dramatic figure of one coming "home" to his own people and being rebuffed is immeasurably enhanced. The story of a returning traveler having the door of home shut in his face evokes our interest and pity; and when a prince comes incognito to his palace and is refused entry, our sympathy grows; but when God Himself bends to human form and makes His way to the people called by His name, the slamming of the door against Him leaves us breathlessly awed. As God, will He force an entry? or call down fire from heaven on His rejectors? As the Son of man, fulfilling the role of both the best and worst treated, He turns away.

Of a returning traveler long since given up for dead, the nineteenth-century poet Tennyson tells the story of *Enoch Arden:*

As children, Philip, Enoch, and Annie were playmates. As they grew up, both Philip and Enoch loved the gentle Annie. She chose the sun-tanned seaman, Enoch, and their marriage, bringing sadness to Philip, gave them immense love and happiness.

51

However, at last hard times forced Enoch to leave his fishing, say farewell to his beloved wife and three dear children, and embark for far shores.

Soon poverty pressed upon Annie, and to add to her sorrow she lost her youngest child. In her distress she accepted the proffered help of Philip, who was by now moderately comfortable, to bring up her boy and girl. The children were soon devoted to him, and Annie was deeply grateful. He loved her still, but not until ten years had passed and Enoch had not returned did he suggest that they become man and wife.

"Wait twelve months more," she pleaded in her loyal love to her husband. And when twelve months had passed, again she deferred a decision. But at last, convinced by a dream that her husband was dead, she agreed to marry. Their home was a comfortable one, and, after the birth of Philip's child, Annie began to forget her first husband.

But what of Enoch? On the homeward journey the ship on which he was sailing was wrecked, and he and two companions drifted to an island "rich, but the loneliest in a lonely sea." First one and then the other of his companions died, and

> Thus over Enoch's early-silvering head
> The sunny and rainy seasons came and went
> Year after year. His hopes to see his own,
> And pace the sacred old familiar fields,
> Not yet had perish'd, when his lonely doom
> Came suddenly to an end.

A ship appeared, and finally he was landed at his home port.

> There Enoch spoke no word to any one,
> But homeward—home—what home? had he a home?

His old home was unoccupied, so he made his way to the tavern where the good-natured but garrulous innkeeper

> Told him, with other annals of the port,
> Not knowing—Enoch was so brown, so bow'd,
> So broken—all the story of his house.

Yearning to see the sweet face of his wife again and to know that she was happy, one evening he looked in a window from behind a tree by Philip's house.

> Now when the dead man come to life beheld

TO JOHN THE BELOVED

> His wife his wife no more, and saw the babe
> Hers, yet not his, upon the father's knee,
> And all the warmth, the peace, the happiness,
> And his own children tall and beautiful,
> And him, that other, reigning in his place,
> Lord of his rights and of his children's love—
> Then he, tho' Miriam Lane had told him all,
> Because things seen are mightier than things heard,
> Stagger'd and shook.

Falling on the earth, he cried to God to uphold him in his loneliness and to give him strength never to let her know or to break into the peace of her and his children.

He kept his word. But another year found him ill and failing. He called his faithful landlady to him and made her swear to keep his secret until he died. Then she might tell them how he died blessing them—"'And say to Philip that I blest him too.'"

> So past the strong heroic soul away.
> And when they buried him the little port
> Had seldom seen a costlier funeral.

Though Enoch's homecoming was a sad one, it was redeemed from utter tragedy by his noble acceptance of what he found and by the lack of treachery in Philip or disloyalty in Annie.

Quite different is the consummation of the journeying of a Greek king, the story of whom was in existence in your day, John, which has come down to our day as a classic, a mixture of legend and history. In it the hero, Odysseus, after many years of hard wandering and adventure, returned at last home. Doubtful of his welcome, an intuition that was soon realized when he found his court filled with drunken carousers and plausible suitors for his wife, he cautiously approached his home halls and incognito addressed an old swineherd.

> To the cottage returning the good old swineherd
> Led him within, and he strewed for a couch soft branches
>   of brushwood,
> Spreading above them the felt of a long-haired goat of
>   the mountains,
> Shaggy and large, that he used for a bed. . . .
>   He in haste with his belt upgirding his tunic
> Went to the yard, where litters of swine were penned in
>   the pig-sties.
> Here two sucklings he chose, and he carried them forth

>   and dispatched them,
> Singed them and cut them in pieces and spitted the flesh
>   on the skewers;
> Then, so soon he roasted it well, to Odysseus he brought it
> Hot on the skewers, with barley-meal all whitely besprinkled.
> Wine then sweet as the honey he mixed in a mazer of ivy,
> Sat him adown confronting his guest and addressed him. . . .
>   And, Odysseus was joyful
> So to be welcomed.

Odysseus, king of Ithaca, was glad of the swineherd's, his lowliest servant's, welcome, for across the way in his palatial home halls a throng of rivals and enemies would greet his unexpected arrival with only hatred, envy, and ill will.

"He [Christ] came unto his own" (K.J.V.).

"He entered his own realm," says *The New English Bible.*

And *The Amplified Bible:* "He came to that which belonged to Him—to His own [domain]."

But the Revised Standard Version says, "He came to his own *home.*"

The poet Robert Frost has Mary pleading with Warren when the worthless hired man turned up yet again, this time ill,

> "Home is the place where, when you have to go there,
> They have to take you in."

And Warren succumbed to Mary's tender plea.

But the Jews didn't take Christ in! They who were His own did not receive Him and did not welcome Him.

And you, John, were not using figurative language when you wrote these words. They were tragically true. "He came unto his own, and his own *received him not*" (K.J.V.).

In Bethlehem's stable no welcome was accorded Him. Officially there was no recognition that the Prince of Peace was born, which is amazing when one reads of the yearning anticipation of Him in the sacred writings of the Jews. Herod's only welcome was callously to unsheathe the sword in defense of his throne.

In Nazareth, Jesus' hometown, the people cast Him out of the synagogue and tried to throw Him over a cliff.

The Gadarenes, who valued pigs more than His presence, in

Jesus came to His own world, but His own people rejected Him.

asking Him to leave their country were probably not the only ones who asked Him to go away. His own words indicate this:

> "Woe to you, Chorazin! woe to you, Bethsaida! for if the mighty works done in you had been done in Tyre and Sidon, they would have repented long ago in sackcloth and ashes. . . . And you, Capernaum, will you be exalted to heaven? You shall be brought down to Hades. For if the mighty works done in you had been done in Sodom, it would have remained until this day" (Matt. 11:21-23).

People were constantly casting Him out of their hearts, until at last He said sadly to His disciples, "Will ye also go away?" (John 6:67, K.J.V.). Even John the Baptist sent his doubtful inquiry. On occasion Jesus' brothers wondered whether He was mad. And in His hour of severe trial one of his disciples betrayed Him, another denied Him, and all forsook Him.

There is, then, great significance in His words " 'He who rejects you rejects me, and he who rejects me rejects him who sent me' " (Luke 10:16).

At last Jerusalem itself rejected Him—Jerusalem, the Holy City of David, whose son and heir He was. Her rulers handed Him over to a hated governor whose hands could perpetrate a shameful death. "We have no king but Caesar' " (John 19:15) was their despicable and treacherous disclaimer. " 'His blood be on us and on our children!' " (Matt. 27:25) was the dreadful curse they called down upon themselves in a frenzy of utter disownership.

That is the story of ultimate rejection. The Son of God was an outcast among His Father's chosen people. Surely this was a situation of historic desperation. Yet there is a saving qualification.

"But *to all who received him*, . . . he gave power to become children of God." There were, then, some who welcomed Him? Who were they? Our curiosity is aroused but not satisfied. Not yet! For, beloved John, all others are but on the periphery of your sight when your vision is focused on Him who is your Light. He is still the theme of your meditation, and His revelation you still pursue.

---

*Jamieson, Fausset, and Brown, *A Commentary on the Old and New Testaments* (Hartford: The S.S. Scranton Co.) vol. 2, p. 128.

CHAPTER VIII

"But to all who received him, he gave power to become children of God; who were born, not of blood nor of the will of the flesh nor of the will of man, but of God."

You were a young man, John, that day you met the Master. You were a very old man when you wrote your Gospel. So perhaps you could write with that excellent combination, the fresh memories of youth and the experience of age. Like that excellence and fascination of which one wrote in admiration of a certain art:

> It is as though innocence and experience were combined, as though a man rich in years, knowledge and ability were looking at the world with the eyes of a child and speaking in the accents of a god.

Whatever it is, there is something about your writing that appeals to youth.

When I was a child and knew almost nothing of the Bible, looking one day through its pages for something to read, I was halted at your first epistle and started to read there, for I could understand these words: "My little children, I am writing this to you so that you may not sin" (chap 2:1). "I am writing to you, little children, because your sins are forgiven" (verse 12).

Loving words of a fond parent, a father in Christ!

In writing these words your pen is dipped into the same ink, as it were, that you used when you wrote in your Gospel of the heritage of the chosen ones: "To all who received him, . . . he gave power to become children of God." You make it very clear, beloved apostle, that this is no natural inheritance; not by flesh, not by one's birth, does it come, but by the grace of Jesus Christ.

This is the mystery of the gospel, and yet it is so simple that the words *children* and *Father* cover our new status. Of course, to be a child one first has to be born, and it is to that starting point in the spiritual life that you go back. "Who were born, not of blood nor of the will of the flesh nor of the will of man, but of God."

There is only one way into physical life, and that is to be born. But of that we have no say. We are but the consequence of causes that involved our parents but predated them as far back as the days when Creation's inexorable laws were laid. What we are by birth, what we have by nature's bestowal, what we obtained by parental heritage, before we meet Christ—these are the factors that determine the course of our natural existence.

If we could start life again we might choose other parents, because from them we derive what we are. We come into the world with nothing not bestowed by them. Concerning such a phenomenal person as Isaac Newton, research has failed to find any link between this genius and his forebears; they were such ordinary people. But we can be sure that from the material of his family background, hidden from human probing, Nature had contrived to produce a wonder-child. And Leonardo da Vinci came from no chosen line. Before he achieved fame, he had often to face the insult and shame of being an illegitimate child, a bastard son.

Not always so kind or capable, it seems, is Mother Nature. If in that tiny cell she sometimes combines the genes to make a genius, sometimes her work produces a moron. Does her hand slip? Perhaps we might beg forgiveness for her, seeing she works with material so infinitesimal that the male seed to people a continent would fit within less than a cubic decimeter. Perhaps! But if it were our child who was "different" (as we say today), or our task was, with endless patience and courage, to train little spastics who drag heavy irons on limbs that should flash by, there might be a tincture of bitterness in our ministry.

Birth is a miracle, but it may be a mockery. The packing together, in so minute a parcel as that invisible cell, of so many qualities and the orderly unfolding of the embryo are two of Nature's masterpieces. But if in that packet there lies locked for us

It is appalling that far from all children being born equally blessed, some have advantages far outweighing those of others.

in the unalterable gene an inferior heritage, life may be an affliction.

We may be well-loved, well-endowed children, or we may be among the unfortunate ones who come into the world, unblessed by Nature or unwelcomed by our parents or the world that receives us. It seems appalling that, far from all little babes being equally blessed, some are loaded with advantages and some are heavily handicapped. Life seems so unfair. Some people have a multitude of gifts and some so few. Some seem to receive all the favors of the world and some all the blows. There seems to be no justice at all in the weighing to us of the talents to assist us through life. And sometimes there seems to be very little mercy. Thus a newspaper editor wrote:

> As we know, life treats some well, and some badly; it is one of the constant amazements of experience that some people get all the breaks, and some the knocks. . . .
> The fact of human inequality cannot be denied or avoided. . . . Every man has worth in himself . . . but it does not follow that all men have the same, or similar, abilities or gifts of grace and character.

In bitterness we might acquiesce to the lines of the infidel Omar Khayyám:

> Into this Universe, and *why* not knowing,
> Nor *whence*, like Water willy-nilly flowing:
>   And out of it, as Wind along the Waste,
> I know not *whither*, willy-nilly blowing.
>
> What, without asking, hither hurried *whence?*
> And, without asking, *whither* hurried hence!
>   Another and another Cup to drown
> The Memory of this Impertinence!"[2]

Yes, we might be tempted to say life is an impertinence, a gross injustice, if it were not, John, for your wonderful words, "Born, not . . . of the will of man, but of God."

Oh, the glorious release of that verse, blessed reversal of all the handicaps of humanity! The priceless paradox: The first shall be last and the last first.

A person may be what people impolitely call a dolt, or (what a wealth there is of invective language) a nitwit, a clod, or as we Australians say, a galah. You may be the child of a murderer or of infamous parents; you may feel that you are weighted down with a thousand encumbrances; you may think you have no gifts, or you may, like the prodigal son, have wasted the lot. You may be unsuccessful or unpopular in your society; you may be unloved or seemingly unlovable, unwanted, and growing hardened in your loneliness. But if you come to Christ He can make you a beloved child of God.

In this new birth we are talking about, all begin equal as children of the Father. Because of our very defects, deficiencies, and handicaps, we will be the objects of more grace, for, to paraphrase a little, where the effects of iniquity abound, grace does much more abound (Rom. 5:20, K.J.V.). It takes more love to stoop lower, and love's glory is to bring back that which is farthest away, to lift up that which has fallen deepest, to win over the most implacable foe, to redeem the most unlikely.

After the new birth comes a new family with God as Father, Jesus as Elder Brother, His Spirit our Comforter, His angels our attendants, His Word our guide, all His followers our brothers and sisters.

God is a watchful, but not overpossessive, Father. Indeed, He allows us so much freedom that sometimes we forget Him. He is protective, but not overwhelming, not stifling, as are some parents. To know the joy of His great fatherhood is to experience an ever-widening and -gladdening aspect of life.

But we could not know or come to God without Christ. "No man cometh unto the Father, but by me (John 14:6, K.J.V.). "No man knoweth . . . the Father, save the Son, and he to whomsoever the Son will reveal him" (Matt. 11:27, K.J.V.). Christ is our Elder Brother, unspeakably understanding of, and sympathetic to, our human nature, for though we are born again, it is an inward more than an outward experience, and, obviously, our natural form still survives. We still may enjoy its legitimate privileges and endure its pains, but our attitudes and responses to them may be modified or may occupy another place in our scale of values after our new experience.

The work of God's Spirit and His holy angels is in the mysterious background of our lives. We see their work, feel their presence, experience their help, but they dwell in the unfathomable abodes of God, too deep for the human senses to perceive, too lofty for mortal experience to become familiar with.

Our new brothers and sisters are both a rich acquisition and a test of faith. In any family we rejoice in the strength and suffer the frailties of the various members. So in this new family of God's household, some will bring to us great joy, and others will be a source of trial.

> In calling God our Father, we recognize all His children as our brethren. We are all a part of the great web of humanity, all members of one family. In our petitions we are to include our neighbors as well as ourselves. No one prays aright who seeks a blessing for himself alone. . . .
>
> God dwells in every abode; He hears every word that is spoken, listens to every prayer that is offered, tastes the sorrows and disappointments of every soul, regards the treatment that is given to father, mother, sister, friend, and neighbor. He cares for our necessities, and His love and mercy and grace are continually flowing to satisfy our need. . . .
>
> If you call God your Father you acknowledge yourselves His children, to be guided by His wisdom and to be obedient in all things, knowing that His love is changeless. You will accept His plan for your life. As children of God, you will hold His honor, His character, His family, His work, as the objects of your highest interest. It will be your joy to recognize and honor your relation to your Father and to every member of His family.[3]

"When my father and my mother forsake me, then the Lord will take me up" (Ps. 27:10, K.J.V.). Even when one has known the reality of this experience, he rejoices in certain of his losses—the loss of care, of fear, of many strivings and envyings, of so many of the perplexing things of life—and he rejoices in the gain of the Father's immeasurable gift of Himself!

But, beloved apostle, to what long musings has your verse led us! Yet how simple is the creed you record: That which is born of the flesh is a sinful man; that which is born of Christ is a spiritual nature, a child of God.

But some of us may take a lifetime to accept it. When will we really believe that we are in the utterly desirable position of being or becoming children in the household of God?

You were one of a family, John, and when you grew older and left the home nest, did you ever wish you were back with Father Zebedee and Mother Salome and the family around the supper table, or chattering in the yard, each at his or her task? While you were, you did not worry unduly about tomorrow, with its need of food, shelter, and clothing. The solid walls of home were about you, a fortress against a sometimes ill or alien world. And within those walls were love, comfort, strength, blessedness, honest labor, cheerful play, and security. You were but a part of the family, and yet you were one to be given pleasure and to be spared pain, one on whom high hopes of the future were being fastened, one who could bring dishonor or fame on those who loved and trusted you.

Just as you experienced that with your own family, so you would teach that we are to be a part of God's family. Our inheritance now is from Him. First a new nature, then as we change, our outer world will bear the print of our transformation. Children of God will not sit down in the dirt of misery and eat the dust of despair. Jesus, having healed the demoniac, clothed him, and the father, after welcoming home the prodigal, dressed him in the best robes.

Then, too, God's children live as from His hand, coveting nothing He would withhold, giving thanks for that which His providence supplies, desiring no more than He would wish them to have.

In your day, John, to get rich quickly you would perhaps have had to resort to brigandage or be cleverly shrewd in some deal. Today some merely have to buy a ticket in a sweepstakes or enter their names for some mammoth commercial handout to receive luck's fortune. Today we can hold in our purse (or better still, bankbook) enough money for bread for the rest of our lives. And not only bread but things you, John, never heard of—radios and phonographs, TV sets, cars, refrigerators, tape recorders, film projectors, and a host of other inventions.

But I hear your caution of extreme simplicity: "Love not the world, neither the things that are in the world. If any man love the world, the love of the Father is not in him (1 John 2:15, K.J.V.). But in what may seem a prohibition, are you not holding out a promise of the greater for the abandonment of the lesser, the joy of taking day by day what the hand of the Father sends to His children?

Of this adoption, Christians today have many comforting assurances:

Those who accept Christ as their personal Saviour are not left as orphans, to bear the trials of life alone. He receives them as members of the heavenly family; He bids them call His Father their Father. They are His "little ones," dear to the heart of God, bound to Him by the most tender and abiding ties. He has toward them an exceeding tenderness, as far surpassing what our father or mother has felt toward us in our helplessness as the divine is above the human.[4]

Another author, whose name I do not know, wrote:

Child of My love, lean hard,
And let Me feel the pressure of thy care;
I know thy burden, child, I shaped it;
Poised it in Mine own hand, made no proportion
In its weight to thine unaided strength;
For even as I laid it on, I said,
I shall be near, and while she leans on Me,
This burden shall be Mine, not hers;

So shall I keep My child within the circling arms
Of My own love. Here lay it down, nor fear
To impose it on a shoulder which upholds
The government of worlds. Yet closer come;
Thou art not near enough; I would embrace thy care
So I might feel My child reposing on My breast.
Thou lovest Me? I knew it. Doubt not then;
But loving Me, lean hard.

On this thought, down the ages have come the wonderful words of St. Paul:

For all who are moved by the Spirit of God are sons of God. The Spirit you have received is not a spirit of slavery leading you back into a life of fear, but a Spirit that makes us sons, enabling us to cry "Abba! Father!" In that cry the Spirit of God joins with our spirit in testifying that we are God's children; and if children, then heirs. We are God's heirs and Christ's fellow-heirs, if we share his sufferings now in order to share his splendour hereafter (Rom. 8:14-17, N.E.B.).

---

[1] Martin Hürlimann, *Athens* (London: Thames & Hudson, Ltd., 1956), p. 9.

[2] Edward FitzGerald (trans.), *Rubáiyát of Omar Khayyám* (first version, 1859).

[3] Ellen G. White, *Thoughts From the Mount of Blessing* (Mountain View, California: Pacific Press Publishing Association, 1956), p. 105.

[4] _____, *The Desire of Ages* (Mountain View, California: Pacific Press Publishing Association, 1940), p. 327.

CHAPTER IX

"The Word became flesh and dwelt among us."

The Word—the Creator, God—became flesh? became man? It is a staggering thought, an incomprehensible statement. One's mote of a mind seems thrown upon a vast sea of timelessness and endlessness. One's little pulsating heart seems shocked to numbness. *God*—eternal, invisible, omnipotent, omniscient, omnipresent—*became flesh*—mortal, material, localized, limited?

John, how could this be? Was He like one of the mythical pagan gods of old? a superman—a little bigger, a little wiser or more cunning, and a *lot* more powerful than ordinary men? There were gods enough already, surely. From your Hebrew reading you would know of Molech, Baal, and Ashtaroth, perhaps of the Egyptian Isis and Osiris. And of the Hindu Buddha you may have heard remotely. There were the host of Roman deities—Apollo, Mars, Mercury, Neptune, Father Jupiter, and the rest. The Greeks had their pantheon of gods and goddesses—Zeus, the father of gods and men, his brother Poseidon, Ares, Aphrodite, Pallas Athena. Each was to be loved or feared, wooed or placated. Some were benign, some awe-inspiring. Some administered justice, some vengeance. Few were dependable, few not capricious. All had proved their worthlessness.

What kind of God is your Word, John? Is He one whom we will approve of, admire, love, obey? Is He one who will satisfy all the heart's yearning that has been in humankind since man first felt more than earthly hunger? Or is He a mere metamorphosis in a

The world has had, and still has, its many gods. Jesus came to show us the true God.

new form? Is He one whom a man feels he can justly worship and lose nothing of his essential manhood, and yet upon whom women can call in their hour of need? Is He one who gives of an overflowing beneficence, or does He exact harsh sacrifices that cause the heart to bleed? What have you to say, John? For upon your answer will depend whether we read a line farther or fling your pages as far as they will go.

So clear and concise is your next statement that its very lack of cluttering explanations encourages us that here is no cloudy ambiguity, no Delphic oracle of hazy meaning, no mere mumblings of confusing intent. It is as clear and beautiful as a diamond, as unadorned, yet sparkling, as a dewdrop in the rising sun. It is something altogether new in the world of religion.

> The Word was made flesh, and dwelt among us, (and we beheld his glory, the glory as of the only begotten of the Father,) *full of grace and truth.* (K.J.V.)

So quietly the sentence lies there, as have millions that have come before and will follow after, that our eye could easily skim across it, leaving us untouched. Yet in it is God's supreme revelation to mankind. A dynamite stick that could shatter a passage through a rock may be nothing but a novel toy to a small boy. A bottle of potent tablets that can work mysterious changes within the human body can be turned over with a gurgle by a pink-fisted little child. So these words for which the ages have waited can be brushed by with apparent impunity or accepted to transform the pathway of humanity.

"The Word was made flesh"! The wonder of this thought was upon you when you wrote your first letter:

> [We are writing] about the Word of Life [in] Him Who existed from the beginning, Whom we have heard, Whom we have seen with our own eyes, Whom we have gazed upon [for ourselves] and have touched with our [own] hands. And the Life . . . was revealed (1 John 1:1, 2, *The Amplified Bible).*
>
> Here was a shatteringly new thing—that God could and would become a human person, that God could enter into this life that we live, that Eternity could appear in time, that somehow the Creator could appear in creation in such a way that men's eyes could actually see Him.
>
> So staggeringly new and unheard-of was this conception of God in a human form that it is not surprising that there were some even in the Church who could not believe it.[1]

And yet this is the reality for which mankind longs, of which a newspaper writer said:

> One of the basic facts of human experience is that personality, hungering for kindred personality, senses personality everywhere.
>
> Even children boggle at the impersonal. They instinctively ascribe thought, sentience, emotion, and purpose to everything. A boy sees nothing ludicrous in issuing commands to his rocking horse; a girl will prattle away to her doll by the hour. . . .
>
> It is a part of man's insatiable hunger for God.

A twentieth-century poet, in summing up his personal beliefs, had this to say:

> I have personally found real help in Galileo's answer to those who thought that the new astronomical universe made the idea of God's care for each of His children impossible: "The sun," he said, "which has all those planets moving around it, can ripen a bunch of grapes as if it had nothing else in the world to do." Why should I doubt the power of that infinitely greater Light?
>
> I believe therefore . . . that it is in the realm of spiritual values, not in the measurements of the material world, that we most nearly realize the nature of that Supreme Being. . . .
>
> The central belief of my religion, in conformity with this, is that the Light has thus shone in our darkness, though the darkness cannot comprehend it. . . . The character of God has been most profoundly revealed to us in the most divine of all personalities, approaching us in history, not through the vague mists of endless time or boundless physical universe.[2]

"Grace and truth"! What do they really mean to us? We have some idea of *truth* and a hazier one of *grace*, and we are weary of words that do not really enlighten us. We have often subscribed to words in searching for light, but not yet have we felt the floodgates of our consciousnesses burst open with complete illumination or our hearts thrill to a Yes! of ringing affirmation. But what have you said, John? "The Word became flesh and dwelt among us, full of grace and truth."

But I can hear your voice, as it were, in ardent zeal hammering upon my brain: "Words! Why do you speak of words? They may be cheap. They may be confusing and confounding. They may go in the ear but never reach the understanding. There are millions of lips to spill and scatter words in every direction. But don't you see that I am speaking of the *Word?* The Word was a life. The things I write aren't empty, idle phrases, but are incarnate in the life of the Word. It is perhaps just as well for me to sometimes say things over in a different way. Do you understand it better in these words: 'Grace and truth came through Jesus Christ'?"

Ah, at last you have named Him, coupling His name with those two attributes. Are they His insignia?

"Grace and truth came through Jesus Christ." Because you have written it, beloved apostle, so naturally, so simply, the heart is flooded with such an infilling of divine love that it does not seem such an utterly incomprehensible thing. Is not every legitimate hunger made for satisfying? Would God create a need that could not be supplied? A longing that must drown? The very desire of the heart bespeaks the evidence of an object of satisfaction. After all, God is not only omnipotent but omnipresent. Could not the Omnipresent One press Himself into tangible and living flesh?

"'Behold, the Lamb of God!'" John the Baptist had cried, directing your eyes, John, toward Him. There was that about Him that made you follow Him, and how soon His presence utterly convinced you of His divinity.

And whether your Master, John, stood, or walked, or sat, or whatever thing He did, He attested His divinity. Perhaps you could best characterize Him in those words *grace* and *truth*, coupling them together, for, unfortunately, something we call grace in human beings may be false, and truth from the human perspective is often graceless. Since His whole life was a portrayal of these attributes, perhaps only as we come to know Him can we really understand the words, "Grace and truth came through Jesus Christ."

---

[1] William Barclay (ed.), *The Gospel of John*, vol. 1, p. 45.
[2] Alfred Noyes, in *This I Believe*, ed. E. P. Morgan (London: Hamish Hamilton, Ltd., 1953), pp. 76, 77.

CHAPTER X

"The only Son from the Father."

In the fourteenth verse of the first chapter of your Gospel, John, the Lord is spoken of as "the only Son from the Father." Again, in the eighteenth verse, He is described as "the only Son, who is nearest to the Father's heart" *(Jerusalem Bible)*. If one had not read the previous Gospels and was new to this story, he would be questioning, "Who was His mother?" for you bring her into the picture only incidentally, not for the purpose of an introduction, but in connection with the wedding of Cana when His first miracle was performed.

To Jesus, John, you were the "friend who sticks closer than a brother" (Prov. 18:24), and it was to you He finally committed His last and chief treasure, His mother.

What it must have meant to you to live with the mother of Jesus during her remaining days, we can hardly imagine. But one thing we can surmise with certainty, that very often you would sit together and talk about Jesus. We can picture you, like an entranced child, sitting by Mary while she told you stories of her Son's early life. Perhaps in time you knew the outline of the stories almost as well as she and would remind her if she omitted a point. But you listened even more keenly if she told any new detail or brought up from the deep wells of memory some long-hidden fact.

How closely your two hearts must have been woven together, drawn by the web of remembrance of One so beloved by both. There was no disloyalty to your own dear mother in your closeness to Mary, who, as the mother of Jesus, was the living repository of all the memories of the Divine Child, Youth, and Man before He gave Himself for His nation and the world. In her uniqueness among all other women she was rival to none.

Strange it seems, then, John, that with your mind and heart a storehouse of treasured stories of the Lord, a source room, as it were, of rare manuscripts, a priceless collection of one-and-only copies, you did not draw on them when you began to write your account of your Lord's life. It seems amazing that you who lived with Jesus' earthly mother so long made no mention of His human generation.

"In the beginning was the Word," you say. "The Word was made flesh" (K.J.V.). Here, humanly and logically, we would expect you to introduce Mary and tell some of the thrilling anecdotes of the Wonder Child.

But you are silent. You lock away your golden hoard into the strongroom of your mind. If any of those wondrous tales attempted to slip from your pen, you sent them tripping back into their pages of memory's manuscripts. Not a word do you say of them, though we await your words. Instead, you sweep by everything of the early decades until you come to Jesus' baptism. Surely, John, this utter silence on so superb a theme must have come only from some compelling veto. Was it a Voice saying to you, "Write not . . ." This silence is profoundly eloquent.

The American author Pearl Buck related an interview with a young Japanese composer:

> "You were born in 1929," I reminded him. . . .
> "Ah, yes, I was born, but I began my life at six years of age, composing and playing the piano."
> "Then?"
> He considered and finally spoke, "I went to the University of Tokyo."
> I was about to inquire, "Nothing between?" and decided not to speak. . . . There was nothing, then, between six and the University of Tokyo.*

Not the number but the significance of experience gives meaning to the years.

Did you somehow feel that on that day of baptism by Jordan's bank not only life began anew for you but, in a significant way, it commenced for Jesus? Did your heart inform you that His existence before that hour of surrender and dedication, prior to the plunging into the waters and the descent of the Dove, was but as a glimmer before the dawn? That it was but the preparation, the setting of the stage, before the play began?

All that went before was essential to Jesus. Mary and Joseph, their family and friends, were all necessary to Him, but it was what followed the baptism that was significant to the world. The hidden years of Jesus were all locked away behind something inexhaustibly vast and wonderful. The bud and blossom of His earthly years had progressed into the fruit.

There is no doubt, John, that by the time you wrote your Gospel you had grown very wise. You knew that people naturally adored the creature more than the Creator. They needed the Word, not the account of the Wonder Child; the baptism more than the Boy.

As for Mary, you knew that they would soon search her out—Mary and the Babe. It would not be hard for them to worship this chosen woman, the mother. Had you experienced, even while Mary lived with you, some transferring of the virtue of the Son to the mother, a venerating of the woman in the flesh, with more than human regard given her as God's chosen vessel?

Perhaps in the earlier months with Jesus, you had been shocked when Mary and Jesus' half brothers had come seeking Him. Instead of going to them with filial affection, He had pointed away from them to His disciples and said, "'Here are my mother and my brothers!'" (Matt. 12:49). And there was the time when a woman had attempted to praise Jesus by blessing the mother who bore Him. But He had gently corrected her: "'Blessed rather are those who hear the word of God and keep it!'" (Luke 11:28). Perhaps at that time you did not understand, but when you wrote your Gospel you did; and you would teach your readers that the new birth eclipses natural birth, that Christ supplies a supernatural one.

With all your love and respect for Mary, you saw that with the baptism her work was done and that she, like all mothers, must drop into the background when her Son left home to take up public office. That Mary found it hard to let her Son go, your narrative reveals. At the wedding at Cana she was still keeping close to Him, and He—still the loving Son that He had always been, though now He had stepped out into the larger family of God—sympathetically heard her request, at the same time gently reminding her of His larger mission.

To you Christ meant a new life, and a new life meant a new birth. Perhaps this is why in your Gospel, rather than writing a chapter on some of Jesus' miracles, you tell of His talk with Nicodemus about being born again. Apparently the new birth loomed large in your thinking, for we find it referred to again in your first epistle: "No one *born of God* commits sin" (chap. 3:9); "For whatever is *born of God* overcomes the world" (chap. 5:4). And so, only as one is born again can he become a child of God. We don't just grow, physically or spiritually, as Topsy, of *Uncle Tom's Cabin* fame, thought:

> "Do you know who made you?"
> "Nobody, as I knows of" said the child, with a short laugh.
> The idea appeared to amuse her considerably; for her eyes twinkled, and she added—
> "I 'spect I growed. Don't think nobody never made me."

Did you already see, John, that many would try to enter the kingdom of your Lord by other than the true door, rebirth? Rebirth to you, we may believe, was as real as your first birth and came by a process as dramatic—a seed sown, its hidden development, the emergence of a new creature. But you are not afraid of the compulsion of this aspect of the gospel: "Ye *must* be born again" (chap. 3:7, K.J.V.). Rather, you are so enamored of the new life that to you the first birth, one's natural entry into life, is, for the child of God, only incidental to the second. It is but the shell that can hold an exquisite pearl.

Therefore, though you loved, respected, and honored Mary, mother of Jesus, never, never by one word would you lift her to that shrine where she would be worshiped as mother of God, at times to the exclusion of her Son. We can be sure that in your Gospel you put Mary right where her Son would wish her to be, and where she herself would desire to be. " 'He must increase, but I must decrease,' " John the Baptist had said (verse 30). Mary too knew how to retire gracefully before the glory of her Son.

---

* *A Bridge for Passing* (London: Methuen & Co., Ltd., 1963), p. 116.

CHAPTER XI

"The next day he saw Jesus."

Many stories begin with "One day . . . " One day! What is that in a lifetime? If you live out the allotted threescore years and ten, you will live about 25,600 days. And what is one day out of so many?

Of the many Christmas cards received over the years, there is one I recollect clearly for the verse it bore:

And yet the joy of one short day
May linger in the heart for aye.

How true that is! The poets have beautifully expressed similar thoughts.

Wrote Shakespeare:

What hath this day deserv'd?
    what hath it done,
That it in golden letters should be set
Among the high tides in the calendar?

And Wordsworth:

One of those heavenly days that cannot die.

Mourned Tennyson:

But the tender grace of a day that is dead
Will never come back to me.

Nostalgically Rupert Brooke mused:

Tenderly, day that I have loved, I close your eyes,
And smooth your quiet brow, and fold your thin dead hands.

TO JOHN THE BELOVED

John the Beloved left his fisherman's trade to follow the Galilean Rabbi.

And the story of your life began, John, one day when something so significant happened that it measured in importance more than a combination of all the days that had gone before. You were a young man at that time and possibly had had the usual escapades and incidents boys and young men of your day encountered. Later your Master nicknamed you and your brother "sons of thunder" (Mark 3:17). Maybe you had your own personal tales of thrilling adventures, exciting encounters and daring sorties. Maybe you and your friends could sit for hours spinning your web of tales, some with breathtaking denouements, and you were not silent among them. But what had gone before, you learned, had happened similarly to many others; even your more rare experiences had happened to a few. There was always somebody to equal or outpace your proud achievements.

And ambition's goal was like a mirage, ever receding on the landscape. But it was a wearying and sometimes futile game, this race to be first, to be best. At times you would far rather have settled down to be just yourself—a loving child, a loyal brother, an obedient and not worthless son to Father Zebedee, and a faithful follower of the true God. Worldly attainments did not naturally appeal to you. You would far rather wander out into the wilderness to find the truth of one, John the Baptist—a prophet, perhaps a dreamer—than to be trying to match or outmatch the up-and-coming young men. And didn't you at last prove that it was in following your natural bent, under the inspiration of your Lord, that your genius lay?

Sighing for something bigger than your little efforts, you were drawn to John the Baptist, a man possessed by a vision that far outreached the stark shadow of his own life. With him you felt your soul expanding.

Then one day it happened, that unique experience so grand, so thrilling, that it seemed you had suddenly awakened to life. I like to think it was on *that* day you first saw Jesus. All that had gone before seemed prelife, a merging into this, a new existence. It appeared to pick you out from all others, even from your brother James, who shared your experience with you. The depths of your being were stirred, as were his, and that was the time when the great Mystery of life entered and the Eternal alone began inhabiting the dwelling place of the inner temple. It lifted you into an experience of such rich awareness that *that day* you marked as the one on which you were reborn. That day you turned from your fisherman's trade to follow the Master.

No wonder that was the day you bring yourself into the story you are unfolding, though you do not name yourself, for with great self-effacement beside so preeminent a Master, you allowed everything personal to retire.

> The next day again John was standing with two of his disciples; and he looked at Jesus as he walked, and said, "Behold, the Lamb of God!"

No wonder you number those first vivid days "the next day," "the next day," "the third day." But you cannot keep that up—there are too many days. And besides, on the day that time began anew for you, you learned the meaning of timelessness. The dominance of hours, days, and weeks as mere units of time fell away under this supreme experience. They became significant to you only because in your memory they were tied to indelible words, unforgettable events, and, among vivid characters, One grandly fadeless.

Yet, John, you did not fail to give those little human, detailed touches of time and place to localize your narrative and mark it with the true ring of authenticity.

What if you had not mentioned that Nicodemus came to Jesus *by night?* Or that it was *midday*, a burning hour, when Jesus sat by the wall of Samaria? And in the inimitable story of the raising of Lazarus, you give precise details: After hearing of Lazarus' sickness, Jesus stayed *two days* where He was and then proceeded to Bethany, about *fifteen furlongs* from Jerusalem, where He found Lazarus had been dead *four days*. But by now the noose of time was catching up with Jesus, and in retrospect you yourself were keenly aware of the tension of outward circumstances, which invaded even the quiet breast of your Lord.

By now you had written what are the first eleven chapters of your book. Then your pen traced the words "Six days before the Passover." Did you then throw down your quill and think, with burning retrospection, "Less than a week!" The last week of your Lord's life before the cross! Your mind again went over what He had said and what He had done. Doubtless at times your hand faltered as you put pen to parchment, and the surface was perhaps smeared with tears. You gazed unseeing into space, sometimes seeing your adored Lord, hearing again that incomparable voice, feeling as though He was only behind the veil of sight or just beyond the verge of sound. The memory quickened, and you repeated with remarkable clarity words He had spoken in those last memorable hours. Your pen raced, and the parchments piled up.

Then, although you had covered so much in eleven chapters, it took ten more to tell as best you could what you wished to say. And at the end you could only write, as if you had done a rather poor job of it, "But there are also many other things which Jesus did; were every one of them to be written, I suppose that the world itself could not contain the books that would be written." But how well you had done, John, the generations until the end of time would bear witness.

And because of what you wrote, others have continued to make your supreme discovery, so that in our day we find one witnessing:

> We have all had in our lives a turning point from which we date everything that happens.
> What, I wonder, was it with you?
> "That was before I met Robert," you hear a woman say, or "Before I took that job," or "Before the baby was born."
> For me, a turning point came when, for the first time in my life, I read the four Gospels through from end to end. It started a new way of thinking and reckoning; it made life curiously rich from that time on. It was like suddenly hearing music and seeing banners.

"Like suddenly hearing music and seeing banners"! Thank God such experiences last more than merely one day. They are lifelong. Edward Wilson—that fine Christian of whom it has been said, "There was from him a radiation of goodness which left an impression deep and lasting" and "Every life he touched was made better and happier for that touch"—wrote in his last message to his wife, "Your little testament and prayer book will be in my hand or in my breast pocket when the end comes. All is well."

CHAPTER XII

" 'Who are you?' "

Did you realize, John, that you would connect your story together by the hooks of question marks?

According to the book of beginnings, the devil asked the first question that led to the downfall of our race. Eve gave a direct reply. Her education had not "advanced" to the place where she had learned to counterplay a question. Being neither deceitful nor yet worldly-wise, she thought of no other than a direct answer. Neither did Adam. When God asked him a question he too gave a straightforward reply. However, their son Cain "developed" beyond their ingenuousness, for when God asked him, " 'Where is Abel your brother?' " he countered, " 'Am I my brother's keeper?' " Since then, Cain's evasive trick has been tried many times, and inconvenient questions have been flicked aside with counter-questions.

Do you realize, John, just what a book of questions yours is? Perhaps you were there when the Jews came to John the Baptist and set the ball rolling with their inquisition " 'Who are you?' "

The Baptist's answers were almost too simple. They merely prompted other questions.

" 'Are you Elijah?' " . . .
" 'I am not.' "
" 'Are you the prophet?' " . . .
" 'No.' " . . .
" 'Who are you?' " they impatiently urged. " 'What do you say

79

Was Pilate really looking for truth when he asked Jesus, "What is truth"?

about yourself?' . . .

" 'I am the voice of one crying in the wilderness, ' " he replied.

They were quieted for a while, but not satisfied. They just did not accept the Baptist's statement; if they had, they would not have been in trouble later when they tried their tactics on Jesus.

" 'By what authority are you doing these things?' " they demanded of Him (Matt. 21:23).

As a teacher, Jesus believed one could not master a more advanced lesson until he had learned the previous one, so He sent them back to their early questioning.

" 'The baptism of John, whence was it? From heaven or from men?' " (verse 25).

They didn't know, or said they didn't know, the answer to that one, so they could advance no further. Actually, at that point they were not looking for truth, any more than Pilate was really looking for truth when he asked Jesus, "What is truth?"

But you, John, have already shown clearly, even here in your first chapter, what Jesus did with questions—honest, sincere questions. He is a good teacher and friend. He does not evade or ignore sincere inquiries. At their very first question John and Andrew learned this. They said, "Master, where do you live?"

There was a world of hospitality in His reply, " 'Come and see.' "

That was one way of dealing with their questions. And whatever other queries they had in mind that day were all transformed into grand assertions and affirmations.

Listen to Andrew after this meeting saying confidently to his brother Peter—and Peter was not the kind of person to whom you took half-baked theories—" 'We have found the Messiah' "!

The same glad certainty takes hold of Philip, who passes the news on to Nathanael: "We have found the Messiah!"

But Nathanael, not having yet seen Jesus, is at the cynical stage, and a cynic, says H. W. Beecher, is "the human owl, vigilant in darkness, and blind to light." So he voices his scornful question, " 'Can anything good come out of Nazareth?' "

But Nathanael's doubts are swiftly swept aside when Jesus greets him, saying, " 'Behold, an Israelite indeed, in whom is no guile!' "

The skeptic now has breath for but one amazed question,

"'How do you know me?'"

The certainty of knowledge in the reply, "'Before Philip called you, when you were under the fig tree, I saw you,'" sweeps into Nathanael a marvelous assurance, and in quiet awe he says, "'Rabbi, you are the Son of God! You are the King of Israel!'"

So questioners and questions arise throughout your book, John. You yourself had your questions, you who leaned on Jesus' breast at the Last Supper and asked that which no other had the courage or closeness to ask.

Doubtless it did not occur to you that you were raising enough queries to put you in a class with the book of Job, that book of questions in what you knew as the Scriptures. When God interposes, as recorded in the thirty-eighth chapter of Job and onward, how He is able to confound man and humble him into a sense of nothingness by question after question! There are at least three dozen questions in 41 verses. Job is overwhelmed and cries, "'I despise myself, and repent in dust and ashes'" (chap. 42:6).

But Jesus came to lift man out of the dust and ashes. He came not only to stir the questions but to satisfy and stimulate with His gracious and illuminating replies. He came not merely to empty man but to refill him; not alone to purge him from his pride but to empower him with a divine passion. He Himself is the answer to the groping mind and perplexed heart. He only can forever set the questing soul at rest.

That this is so, your story in the sixteenth chapter clearly reveals. There you show Jesus as a wonderful friend and teacher. You show Him as one expecting questions, reading unspoken questions, promising answers from the highest Source of authority.

Now, we know certain things about a normal curiosity. In children it is an "appetite for knowledge" one writer said. "Curiosity," said Samuel Johnson, "is one of the permanent and certain characteristics of a vigorous mind." And curiosity prompts questions. As R. L. Stevenson said, "You start a question, and it is like starting a stone. You sit quietly on the top of a hill; and away the stone goes, starting others."

Those who have had to do with young children may have their own version of this simple illustration from Elizabeth Goudge:

> His whole body seemed at times to be curved into the shape of a

question-mark and the word "why" was seldom off his lips. . . .
"Why don't you grow a beard?" he asked Jocelyn.
"I've been a soldier," said Jocelyn, "and in the Army it is the fashion to have a moustache only!"
"Why?"
"To distinguish soldiers from sailors, who are either cleanshaven or have beards."
"Why?"
"It's just the fashion."
"Why?"
"I don't know."
"Why don't you know?"[1]

At times it is but natural for questions to be asked. The more that is unknown, the more one would expect questions to be asked of some authority. A speaker, at the conclusion of a talk, may be highly flattered or deeply discouraged if no questions are asked. Either he has made his subject perfectly clear and told everything his hearers wished to know or he has failed to arouse in them a desire to know more.

A teacher told me of a lecture he gave to some members of a brotherhood. They were all migrants, and he was to talk to them of the history of the country to which they had come, a subject in which he was well versed. So that he would not be interrupted, he asked his listeners at the beginning to save any questions they might have until the conclusion of the session, when they would be given opportunity to speak. At the end of the talk the teacher asked whether there were any questions. A deep silence followed, and then without a word the whole class rose and filed out of the room. The speaker was most disconcerted. Could they not understand him? Had he failed to interest them? What impression had he made on his hearers? An explanation from a superior of the brotherhood partly set his mind at rest, though it did not answer his own wondering—the whole group was under a vow of silence.

During His last hours before the cross, when Jesus was telling His disciples about the future, He knew He was speaking of what to them was a profound mystery. Did you, John, sense the tinge of disappointment in His words " 'But now I am going to him who sent me; yet none of you asks me, "Where are you going?" ' " (John 16:5). Weren't you all so plunged into sadness by His talk of going away that you forgot to ask the question that concerned Him,

" ' "Where are *you* going?" ' " That was the most vital question you could have asked, yet humanly you were all locked into your forebodings and didn't ask it.

Some things Jesus wants us to ask. How glad we can be of this! He doesn't want us to go through the world unquestioning, blindly accepting what is told us, never opening our minds to broader and deeper aspects. Is Jesus upset when we examine our faith? There is a refusal to ask questions that savors of bigotry. The poet Siegfried Sassoon has put it tersely:

> I'm amazed at folk
> Drinking the gospel in and never scratching
> Their heads for questions.

Jesus is not afraid for us to ask questions. Sometimes we—especially children—do not like to be questioned. We fear to disclose our ignorance or what the reply will reveal. But Jesus is not like that. He welcomes them—honest questions. " 'None of you asks me,' " He gently rebuked.

Sometimes, too, we do not like to ask questions because we are afraid of the answers, or we fear to approach the one from whom we would inquire, or our relationship closes our lips. One of Pearl Buck's characters, a Dr. MacLeod, says in reply to a question about his Chinese wife, " 'I did not ask. We were never close enough for questions.' "

In our century many have known the terrible ordeal of political interrogations or national inquisitions. The answers given could lead to or away from a gas chamber, or standing against a wall with those to be shot, or being sent to an internment camp or into exile or to some other terrible fate. And not only has being questioned been dangerous but some have known that their safety lay in not asking about certain things, the meaning or knowledge of them being better left in the dark. Also, to ask questions that might stir people from their ease or apathy could stigmatize one as a fomenter of trouble, a revolutionary.

But in everyday life, questions are important, and today, John, the pertinence of questions is as alive as in your day, and we can understand the diffidence of the disciples as unfolded in your story:

> Some of his disciples said to one another, "What is this that he says

to us, 'A little while, and you will not see me, and again a little while, and you will see me'; and 'because I go to the Father'?" They said, "What does he mean by 'a little while'? We do not know what he means" (John 16:17, 18).

And all were too afraid to ask. But Jesus, like a wise, kind teacher with a class of muddled children, understood. How beautiful are your words, John, replete with the understanding of the Lord:

> Jesus knew that they wanted to ask him; so he said to them, "Is this what you are asking yourselves, what I meant by saying, 'A little while, and you will not see me, and again a little while, and you will see me'?" (verse 19).

For the disciples' future reference, Jesus went much further than merely answering the present questions. He provided for the day when He would not be with them and directed them to Him to whom He was going and at whose right hand He would sit:

> "Hitherto you have asked nothing in my name; ask, and you will receive, that your joy may be full. . . . In that day you will ask in my name; and I do not say to you that I shall pray the Father for you; for the Father Himself loves you, because you have loved me and have believed that I came from the Father. I came from the Father and have come into the world; again, I am leaving the world and going to the Father" (verses 24-28).

And now, in understanding and grateful humility, the disciples came to a glad acclamation:

> "Now we know that you know all things, and need none to question you; by this we believe that you came from God" (verse 30).

How glad we can be for the settlement of questions, and with such wonderful assurance!

Here is a modern testimony:

> If I were a dictator the first book I would burn would be the Bible. . . .
> When Jesus chose twelve men to be with Him and carry on His mission after He was gone He didn't select a group of rubber stamps.

There was Peter, the impetuous; Andrew the plodder; John, the poet; Simon, the fiery zealot; Thomas, the melancholy. They were not stereotyped "yes" men. He put a premium on their infinite variety. They were united by their very differences. He encouraged them to question His most fundamental beliefs and in open discussion their doubts were resolved and their faith strengthened.

You don't have to read political science or study constitutional law to understand democracy or to realize that, when originality is thwarted, progress is halted. You only have to read the Bible to provide understanding. . . . From the point of view of a dictator who can rule only as long as individual thoughts and ideas and conduct are suppressed, these are dangerous thoughts to be lurking in the mind of man. Yes, if I were a dictator the first book I would burn would be the Bible.[2]

---

[1] *A City of Bells* (London: Gerald Duckworth & Co., Ltd., 1938). .
[2] Quentin Reynolds, in *This I Believe*, ed. E. P. Morgan, pp. 174, 175.

CHAPTER XIII

When you were an old man, John, did your memories sometimes grow dim, or did you live with them with more clarity than the reality of the present? Did you ever feel, My memory is so bad that sometimes I forget my own name? We may laughingly accuse you of this when you wrote of "that disciple whom Jesus loved." Rather, perhaps, using the words of the poet Samuel Rogers, we may lovingly picture you and your

> Sweet Memory! wafted by thy gentle gale,
> Oft up the stream of Time I turn my sail.

How we would like to have made that journey with you! Failing this, how we puzzle by what process you recalled with such detail the words and incidents of so long ago in your life. How was it you could repeat so much of what your Teacher had said? You must have been a most attentive listener and gifted with a remarkable memory. But it is useless for us to try to separate natural talents from spiritual endowments in a work in which both had their part.

We know that the school lessons of boys of your day were largely the repeating of Scripture, so the power and use of memory were well developed. As Leslie Weatherhead wrote:

> An Eastern Jewish memory was a far more reliable instrument than a Western modern one. For instance, one reads that every Jew knew the Psalter in Hebrew by heart and many passages of the Law as well.... In our Lord's day spoken words would be remembered with far greater accuracy than they would today.[1]

Of Arab people still living in patriarchal simplicity near the home country of our Lord, Siegfried H. Horn has written:

> Repeatedly when sitting in a Bedouin camp I was amazed at the fabulous memory of my illiterate Arab hosts who could tell stories of tribal warfare that had taken place many generations ago. I was equally surprised to find them capable of recalling their genealogies for centuries, listing their ancestors by name in an unbroken sequence. I could not help making comparisons between my Arab friends and the patriarchs who had handed down historical information for centuries in an oral form without corrupting it.[2]

The nature of memory is unknown, Dr. Alexis Carrol has said:

> From time to time people refer to "photographic memory." . . . By this term is meant, presumably, the ability to image an absent scene with all the vividness, distinction and detail of a photographic print. . . .
>
> Does there . . . exist anything to correspond with the popular notion of "photographic memory"? . . . The answer is clearly in the negative. . . . Exactly how this reconstructing of the past is achieved is the chief mystery of memory. It is a mystery which psychology has failed to dispel. Perhaps it is a mystery which will never yield up its secrets.[3]

Thus, like many other mysteries, we can only accept and not explain memory's demonstration. Its power has been evident to a remarkable degree in some.

> In ancient times Themistocles grew high in the popular esteem when it was realized he knew all the 20,000 citizens of Athens by name, while Cyrus could call by name all the soldiers in his vast army. Ben Jonson could remember every word he had ever written as well as whole books by other authors which he had read. Rev. John Beale, sometime Chaplain to Charles II, could memorize the contents of any book he had ever read after a single reading. . . .
>
> Seneca the Elder could repeat 200 long poems at a moment's notice, and could say them backwards or forwards at will. Dr. Sanderson, Bishop of Lincoln, knew great chunks of the classics by heart, while one Joseph Scalinger committed to memory the whole of Homer in three weeks. Macaulay learned vast quantities of books and verse without effort; to know the whole of "Paradise Lost" by heart was nothing to him.
>
> Bishop Jewel could repeat anything he had penned after once reading it, and anything he had once read, no matter what out-of-the-ordinary or foreign words it contained, forwards or backwards without hesitation. . . .
>
> Thomas Fuller had so capacious a memory of this kind that he

could recite in order all the shop signs that hung on both sides of the road from the beginning of Pastornoster Row at Ave Maria Lane to the bottom of Cheapside. And he could also dictate to five shorthand writers at the same time on so many different subjects, without getting confused.[4]

This quotation deals with notable people, but those whose paths lead them along the highways and byways encounter in all walks of life individuals who seem to be endowed with amazing memories. Ion Idriess, an Australian writer, has remarked how sometimes he had been surprised when camping at night to find a swagman (Americans might call him a hobo) who "could reel off the classics and was familiar with ancient and modern history and with other interests."

Of the selectiveness of memory, a visitor to the isolated island community of Pitcairn wrote:

> Both men and women have a phenomenal memory when anything dealing with ships and the sea is involved. On other topics—local history, dates, events, local origin of words or customs—they seem to be curiously forgetful. But the visits of liners, warships, freighters, and yachts remain stamped indelibly in their minds long after the event. At one social evening, the maritime traffic of ten, twenty, even thirty years in the past was being recalled by a group of islanders. As each ship's name was mentioned, those in the room remembered exactly who had disembarked or taken passage on her, what major cargo had been offloaded, the sea conditions at the time, what dunnage the captains had put over the side for them to use as lumber, the moods of the captains, and so on.[5]

We are inclined to remember things we are interested in—the greater the interest, the more we will give our full attention.

I recall a lecturer, whose own memory was so good that in an examination he had quoted the textbook so fully and accurately that the examiners had accused him of cheating, telling of being amazed at two workmen on a train in which he was traveling. They were discussing the winners of the Melbourne Cup, and could reel off the names of the horses who had won, going back through the years and matching horse with year. This was an exercise not deliberately learned, but could be credited to interest alone. No doubt many of us could name people inferior or ordinary in general knowledge, yet who have a detailed and extensive knowledge of something that grips their enthusiasm.

When Jesus spoke, John was ever the careful listener.

When Jesus spoke in the great auditorium of the out-of-doors or with your small, intimate group, you, John, were no doubt the careful listener and your mind was the impressionable wax on which His words were recorded as by an incisive needle.

In the modern research of the problem of learning, one point at least might illuminate our present subject:

> In memorizing any sort of material which is to be reproduced, the effectiveness of repeated reading, listening, or looking is enhanced by recitation. . . . By reciting, the learner performs just those activities which will be required of him later.[6]

We can reasonably imagine the words of the beloved Master, whose voice was no more heard, whose lips were unseen, were repeated over and over in the mind of His devout disciple, in a less literate age than ours, when the oral word was newspaper, gossip column, storybook, and textbook in one. And we can imagine how frequently they were repeated to individuals or groups of interested listeners.

Coming very close to our own day, we find this comment:

> A good many years ago, when I was a reporter, I was suddenly packed off to interview Lord ——— about some political matter. Before leaving I looked him up in *Who's Who* and discovered that he . . . was now nearly ninety. . . .
>
> At first my worst fear seemed to be confirmed. For though nobody could have been more charming or more courteous, his mind was quite definitely elsewhere. It was in fact solely absorbed in the destruction of flies. . . .
>
> And then, quite suddenly, he paused against the sunlit window. A light came into his eyes. His voice gathered power. "I remember a speech by Disraeli," he muttered. He cleared his throat. He began to repeat the speech. He went on for nearly ten minutes. It was an astonishing feat. And then quite suddenly he stopped, sank onto the window seat, and lifted a feeble hand to flick a fly.
>
> "And what," you may ask, "has this to do with the Gospel according to St. John?"
>
> It has this to do with it. St. John was a very old man when the Gospel was first given to the world.[7]

The implication is that, though it may be a remarkable feat, it is no impossible act for an old man to repeat word for word oratory vividly impressed upon his mind in earlier days.

Also close to our own times there is the example of Nadezhda Mandelstam. For nineteen years she had been the wife of Osip Mandelstam, Russia's greatest poet in this century, and his widow for forty-two years, much of which time she spent fleeing from place to place. She was also a close friend of the poet Anna Akhmatova. At the age of 65, Nadezhda Mandelstam wrote two volumes of memoirs, which were published in the West.

Joseph Brodsky, who came to know her, wrote:

> Poetry always precedes prose, and so it did in the life of Nadezhda Mandelstam, and in more ways than one. As a writer, as well as a person, she is a creation of two poets with whom her life was linked inexorably: Osip Mandelstam and Anna Akhmatova. . . . What strengthened the bond of that marriage as well as of that friendship was a technicality: the necessity to commit to memory what could not be committed to paper, i.e., the poems of both authors. . . .
>
> Repeating day and night the words of her dead husband was undoubtedly connected not only with comprehending them more and more but also with resurrecting his very voice, the intonations peculiar only to him, with a however fleeting sensation of his presence. . . . The same went for the poems of the physically often absent Akhmatova, for once set in motion this mechanism of memorization won't come to a halt. . . .
>
> And gradually those things grew on her. If there is any substitute for love, it's memory. To memorize, then, is to restore intimacy. Gradually the lines of those poets became her mentality, became her identity. They supplied her not only with the plane of regard or angle of vision; more important, they became her liguistic norm. . . . The clarity and remorselessness of her pages, while reflecting the character of her mind, are also inevitable stylistic consequences of the poetry that had shaped that mind.[8]

As Joseph Brodsky has so sensitively described the process that went on in the mind and life of Nadezhda Mandelstam, could it not have been that a similar recapitulation of occasion, words, expression, et cetera, of his beloved Master was the experience of "that disciple whom Jesus loved"?

But no matter how we may compare and conjecture, we will never understand your masterpiece, John. We can only be grateful for the findings of scholars and lovers of your Gospel, and ponder over such commentaries as this:

> The more we know about the fourth Gospel the more precious it becomes. For seventy years John had thought of Jesus. Day by day the

Holy Spirit had opened out to John the meaning of what Jesus said. So when John was near the century of life, and when his days were numbered, he and his friends sat down to remember.... There were many things which seventy years ago he had not understood; there were many things which in the seventy years the Spirit of Truth had revealed to him. These things John set down even as the eternal glory was dawning upon him. So then when we read this Gospel let us remember that we are reading the Gospel which of all the Gospels is most the work of the Holy Spirit, speaking to us of the things which Jesus meant, speaking through the mind and memory of John the Apostle.[9]

---

[1] *Over His Own Signature* (London: The Epworth Press, 1955).

[2] *Signs of the Times*, June, 1957 (U.S.A. edition).

[3] Ian M. Hunter, *Memory: Facts and Fallacies* (New York: Penguin Books, Inc., 1957), pp. 146, 152.

[4] David Gunston, "Memory Magicians," in *Pitman's Shorthand Teacher's Supplement*.

[5] Ian M. Ball, *Pitcairn: Children of Mutiny* (Boston: Little, Brown and Company, 1973), pp. 232, 233.

[6] Ian M. Hunter, *op. cit.*, p. 146.

[7] Beverly Nichols, *The Fool Hath Said* (London: Jonathan Cape, Ltd., 1936), pp. 119, 120.

[8] Joseph Brodsky in *New York Review of Books*, republished in *The AGE Monthly Review*, Melbourne, Australia, September, 1981.

[9] William Barclay (ed.), *The Gospel of John*, vol. 1.